DEAD RECK

I0190809

A Review of Horror and the Weird in the Arts
Edited by Alex Houstoun and Michael J. Abolafia

No. 30 (Fall 2021)

DEAD RECKONINGS is published by Hippocampus Press, P.O. Box 641, New York, NY 10156 (www.hippocampuspress. com). Copyright © 2021 by Hippocampus Press. Cover art by Jason C. Eckhardt. Cover design by Barbara Briggs Silbert. Hippocampus Press logo by Anastasia Damianakos. Orders and subscriptions should be sent to Hippocampus Press. Contact Alex Houstoun at deadreckoningsjournal@gmail.com for assignments or before submitting a publication for review.

ISSN 1935-6110   ISBN 978-1-61498-355-2

And I, for One, Welcome Our New Insect Overlords

Daniel Pietersen

DAISY BUTCHER and JANETTE LEAF. *Crawling Horror: Creeping Tales of the Insect Weird*. London: British Library Publishing, 2021. 320 pp. £8.99 tpb. ISBN 9780712353496.

To any external observer, some indifferent alien surveyor, it would be the insects who rule the planet known as Earth. They fill the gamut of ecological niches, from lowly grazer to apex predator. They've developed agriculture and architecture as well as less visible, but no less complex, social structures. They outnumber the planet's dominant mammalian species, an amusingly recent development in its bio-history, by a factor of nearly 1.5 billion to one.

Yet to us, those arriviste mammals, they are little more than creepy-crawlies; at best considered jewels to be collected, at worst as vermin to be eradicated. In this anthology for the British Library's Tales of the Weird series, Daisy Butcher and Janette Leaf have collected a series of stories that do what horror does best: turn the tables on our assumptions. What if we become the jewels, they ask. What if we become the vermin?

What if we become the food?

Even in a collection noted for its striking design, *Crawling Horror*'s cover immediately impresses. The skull on the back of a death's-head hawk-moth leers out at us in a sickly blue-green, the moth's winglets creating an ornate shroud draped around its shoulders. Yet, despite this grisly motif and its inescapable association with *The Silence of the Lambs,* the hawk-moth is a perfectly harmless creature. It is nothing more than our prejudice and superstition that have cursed the moth with an evil omen, even to the extent of the species' formal, scientific names; atropos, lachesis, and styx. This prejudice, and the fear that arises from it, are outlined in a number of the stories in *Crawling Horror*.

Indeed, the book opens with Edgar Allan Poe's "The Sphinx," where the narrator, already highly strung after fleeing an outbreak of cholera, seems to see "some living monster of hideous conformation" with a "representation of the Death's Head, which covered nearly the whole surface of its breast." This vision creates "a feeling of horror and awe—with a sentiment of forthcoming evil, which I found impossible to quell by any effort of reason"; and, as the beast opens its jaws to screech, "a sound so loud and expressive of woe, that it struck upon my nerves like a knell," the narrator faints clean away. An astute reader will guess the twist of this very short piece fairly easily, but it is still unsettling when it comes—a reminder that fear can make us see what we think we should see, rather than what is really there. It is a motif that recurs through *Crawling Horror,* not least in the pomposity of the Reverend James Milligan in "An Egyptian Hornet." Here Algernon Blackwood gives us a character study of hypocrisy and cowardice as the reverend pours his own venom and untrustworthiness onto the motionless figure of a hornet, even as he admits that its "shiny body was beautiful, and the yellow stripes on its sleek, curved abdomen were like the gleaming ornaments upon some feminine body of the seductive world he preached against." Milligan is entranced by the insect as much as he is repelled by it, something I think many of us have felt and an example of that "aversion with a backward glance, lingering over and even savouring its subject" that the philosopher Carolyn Korsmeyer calls the sublate.

Not satisfied with these intimate, one-on-one encounters, Butcher and Leaf have also expanded their vision to the inevitable result of prejudice and confusion: open conflict. In Carl Stephenson's "Leiningen versus the Ants" we see the colonizer—a white plantation owner in Brazil—stare into the mandibles of the jungle's response to that colonisation: a migration of ferocious, all-consuming ants. Rather than flee, Leiningen makes a stand, fueled first by stubbornness and then by desperation, and deploys fire and gasoline against the horde. It is hard not to root for the ants given Leiningen's unpleasant arrogance, perhaps not Stephenson's intent, but there is also a chill as the mass of insects inch toward their enemies. "They're over," cries one of Leiningen's laborers, and the following scene is as disturbing as it is brief. Greater even than this is "The Miracle of the Lily" by Clare Winger Harris, an astonishing piece of speculative horror that spans generations and millennia in its description of a global conflict between insects and humans. Published in 1928, "The Miracle of the Lily" presages modern-day concerns about ecological collapse: "There was not enough food to feed the people of the earth. Fruit and vegetables were becoming a thing of the past," laments one of the story's multiple narrators, only to be corrected by a descendant who admits that "the fault was not with Nature but with man's economic system." The planet's surface is reduced to a barren wasteland and humanity clings to isolated settlements built around the oxygen processors that keep them alive in the absence of vegetation. This is a gloomy, cynical tale that allows the possibility of optimism only to deny it at the last moment, but I found it deeply emotional and timely. A warning for the future from the past.

My favorite piece in this anthology, though, is the one I find most deeply disturbing. In "Caterpillars" E. F. Benson takes the least threatening aspect of the insect's life-cycle, the defenseless and squirming grubs, and focuses in on their "irregular lumps and swellings," the "soft fleshy thud" as they fall to the floor. In contrast with the pleasant setting, a few days' holiday in a friend's villa, there is something about the faceless, implacable threat with which Benson infuses these lumps of flesh—"or whatever it is that caterpillars are made of"—that I find deeply, inexplicably unpleasant. When the narrator stumbles upon them and "then, as I looked, it seemed to me as if they all suddenly became conscious of my presence," I squirm and itch, no matter how clearly I know it's coming. There is a vileness to their strange, abject existence that is almost zombie-like and, as the story eventually reveals, infectious.

Although these few are standouts in the book, *Crawling Horror*'s other tales of cursed beetles and protective butterflies are all enjoyable, especially when taken as a way of re-examining our own place in a world where we are, at least numerically, very much a minority. Even the book's pages, scattered with small but wonderfully detailed illustrations of bees and ants and all their kin, remind us of how perilous our existence would be if, to paraphrase another of Benson's chilling phrases, "all the mouths were turned in our direction."

An excellent addition to an already excellent series from co-editors Butcher and Leaf.

The World and Works of R. Murray Gilchrist: An Interview with Daniel Pietersen

Alex Houstoun

I do not recall how I first came across the works Robert Murray Gilchrist (1867–1917). I know that in January 2011 I had purchased a short story collection, *The Basilisk and Other Tales of Dread* (Ash-Tree Press, 2003), based on something I had read somewhere, and was meekly trying to pitch the small publishing house I interned at that Gilchrist would be an author worth considering for a series it was preparing to launch focusing on overlooked and under-appreciated works. While I was partially motivated in the hope that the publisher would reimburse me the cost of the book I had bought—I was an unpaid intern and the five days of the week not spent at the publisher's office were spent working at a coffee shop that, to this day, I irrationally dislike—I was also deeply struck by the Gilchrist stories I had read.

To read them was to give myself over wholly to the words on the pages and the settings therein and then find myself in a mental fog after setting the book down. I found myself reacting in a way similar to when I read Lovecraft for the first time; overwhelmed and confused by all that seemed to be happening—or all that was not happening but, perhaps, being perceived—and yet deeply drawn to the feeling of confusion and sensation that I was drowning in the author's words and the uncanny worlds—ours but not ours—that his hapless characters found themselves in. There is a dreamlike, unreal quality to Gilchrist's stories unlike much else I have read. If one were to put genre labels on it, I suppose I would say that his work occupies an interesting position of being not Gothic and not being weird as the genre came to be understood in the early twentieth century. Gilchrist feels somewhere distinctly separate while incorporating aspects of both genres. Perhaps he is a bridge between the two . . . perhaps he is something like an interesting detour.

I never made much of an effort to learn more about Gilchrist as an author and, following a few unsuccessful attempts at finding other books collecting his works, simply assumed that *The Basilisk* would remain something of an oddity on my shelf that I would pick up from time to time for a single story or two.

This is all to say that learning that about the recent publication of *I Am Stone: The Gothic Weird Tales of R. Murray Gilchrist* was a most welcome surprise. That the collection is edited by Daniel Pietersen, someone we have had the distinct pleasure of working with and publishing for a few years now, was a special bonus. Daniel was kind enough to discuss Gilchrist's life and work over a series of emails.

AH: For better or worse, I think I have to start this conversation by saying that there is a bit of Gilchrist history between us and how excited I am, finally, to have a real excuse to speak at length about him and his work.

The first piece you wrote for *Dead Reckonings* in 2017, and one of the very first pieces, if not the first, I read as an editor of this journal, was on Gilchrist. In that initial pitch email you wrote that Gilchrist has a "poetical vision, overlaying his love of landscape . . . where characters slide in and out of time and space." You then added that, as far as you were aware, there is "little discussion of this aspect of his work."

Can you explain how you first came to read Gilchrist and what has led you, thus far, to bring him into the discussion and champion his work?

DP: I first discovered Gilchrist, like a lot of things that become obsessions, completely by accident. I picked up *A Night on the Moor and Other Tales of Dread,* the collection of his weird tales that Wordsworth Editions published in 2006, at a secondhand bookshop. That was probably ten, maybe even fifteen years ago. I'm hazy on the times as I'm sure I got around to reading the book long after I bought it. I was immediately struck by stories such as "The Crimson Weaver" and "The Return," with their eerie take on vampire lore, but also disappointed that the book contained no real information on Gilchrist himself beyond a few lines in the back cover's promotional blurb. After that I made intermittent attempts to find out more about Gilchrist as a person. I found a few articles by Laurence Bush, including an insightful essay in the *Wormwood* journal, and then discovered the existence of the Ash Tree Press edition of his works (*The Basilisk and Other Tales of Dread*) that was published in 2003 (effectively the same stories as in the Wordsworth collection but with a bibliographical introduction that sheds some light on who Gilchrist was a person, at least through the eyes of friends and scholars). I think what drew me in most, though, is the photograph on his Wikipedia page, one of two I've been able to find, which shows a man who looks absolutely terrified by the things he has dreamt of.

After that it just became a puzzle to try and put together. He'd written so much but all of it, even the few modern reprints, was hard to get hold of or simply no longer available. Every now and then I'd speak to someone who'd say they'd read one of his stories, normally "The Crimson Weaver," or I'd find a new piece of information on the web and that would be enough to keep me searching. It seemed such a shame that someone who'd spent his life writing was now lost, especially as I increasingly began to realize that his work formed a bridge between earlier Decadent or Gothic works and what we now think of as weird fiction. When I finally read Hugh Walpole's memoir *The Apple Trees,* which contains some fragments about his friendship with Gilchrist, and saw his wistful hope that "someone soon will rediscover [Gilchrist], as others far less worthy than he have been rediscovered," then I knew I at least had to try and get it done!

AH: I find the photograph you refer to quite fascinating. The camera is positioned below Gilchrist so he is looking down at the viewer and, as you note, his gaze is rather intense. He looks possibly scared or haunted but also as if he is about to tell you one hell of a wild story. On a lighter note, I find his hair oddly distracting as it appears . . . wet? Did he just come in from the rain? Is he drenched in sweat after some sort of fright or exertion? It adds to the sort of otherness or surreal, unknown nature of Gilchrist.

It's odd, I usually get annoyed when folks baselessly speculate about Lovecraft's life and the type of person he was—insisting he was a recluse or a deeply angry, misanthropic person his whole life or whatever nonsense people say online. And yet, here I am indulging in similar behavior and allowing my imagination to run wild with a single photograph of Gilchrist. I think part of my frustration may stem from the fact that, with Lovecraft, there is so much material readily available with which one can educate oneself—there's really no excuse, to a degree, for being ignorant about Lovecraft. On the other hand, there seems to be surprisingly little about Gilchrist.

Your introduction is very upfront about this and you open rather bluntly with "We know frustratingly little about the life of Robert Murray Gilchrist." You provide some rather nice quotations from the aforementioned Walpole memoir—I am quite fond of the rather romantic line "He liked candles and Elizabethan thickness of atmosphere and, if possible, the rain beating on the leaded panes"—but very little else by way of Gilchrist's own history or life. At the risk of having you repeat the introduction's opening line, is there really such little information about Gilchrist? Do the Laurence Bush articles and Ash-Tree Press edition you refer to offer anything else to provide a slightly clearer picture of Gilchrist as a person?

DP: Yes, he does look weirdly damp. He looks equally disheveled in the only other photo I've found of him, and it's quite a marvel that these aren't just random snaps but official photographs that were used to advertise his books. Maybe the effect was intended, who can say?

In answer to your question I'm afraid the answer is yes, there's very little information about Gilchrist as a person. In his *Wormwood* article Bush states that "no biography of Gilchrist exists" and this is corroborated in the introduction to *The Basilisk* when John Pelan and Christopher Roden bemoan that "of biographical information on Robert Murray Gilchrist, there is little to be had." There's no primary source material, preferably letters or other biographical writings in his own hand, beyond that which we can glean from the public record; Gilchrist was born in 1867 to Robert and Isabella Murray Gilchrist, he had two sisters (an elder sister Jane and the younger Isabella), he trained and worked as a cutler but abandoned that at an early age in favor of writing, and he died suddenly of pneumonia in 1917. All we do know of him are from secondary sources such as the memoirs of people like Hugh Walpole, which are quoted at length in both Bush's article and the Ash-Tree edition (and my own book!), and letters from friends and acquaintances. My favorite of these, which seem not to have been picked up elsewhere although I do refer to them in my introduction to *I Am Stone,* are the letters sent to Gilchrist by the Scottish poet and novelist William Sharp. These grow from relatively formal to more chatty and show that the two were sincere friends. Gilchrist's father was born in Scotland, so this may have helped the kinship between them. I need to do more dedicated research into these letters as they seem to offer the nearest we have to a timeline of Gilchrist's life, albeit a one-sided one. After Gilchrist's lifetime there are occasional pieces in local-interest journals and newsletters, largely ones related to Derbyshire history, but little more than conjecture. The only other real source we have are reviews of Gilchrist's writing, although they are by default written through the lens of the reviewer and can lead to confusion; for example, Bush claims that an 1890 review of Gilchrist's debut novel refers to it as "weird horror," which must be an early use of the term, but I sadly can't find this quotation when reading the actual review. Maybe Bush has confused his references or it's simply wishful thinking.

AH: Whether or not Gilchrist's first novel, *Passion the Plaything* (1890), was actually referred to as "weird horror" at the time of publication, you present some other choice reviews that foreshadow a bit of the work that Gilchrist is best known for now. The *Literary World* described the novel as "crude and unnatural" and the *Spectator* found it to be "an unpleasant book, containing far too much in the way of sensuous descriptions." To be clear, it is the "unnatural" and "sensuous descriptions" that one would positively associate with Gilchrist—I certainly do not mean to suggest that he is known as being crude and writing unpleasant reading material!

This reputation is then firmly established with the 1894 publication of his short story collection *The Stone Dragon and Other Tragical Romances*. Gilchrist's publisher described the collection as "a volume of stories of power so weird and original as to ensure them a ready welcome," and you quote a reviewer for the *Academy* declaring: "There is nothing quite like *The Stone Dragon* in modern English fiction: but in it you may distinctly trace the influence of Poe, and perhaps also of Villiers de l'Isle-Adam and Charles Baudelaire."

The entire contents of *The Stone Dragon* are included in *I Am Stone*. This is a rather large, open-ended question, but can you speak to the importance of *The Stone Dragon* both as a work in its own right and what it may have meant to Gilchrist? It comes four years after Gilchrist's first novel; does it show him coming into his own as a writer? Or is it, as you say in the introduction, a work of greater importance in how it predates weird fiction and allows us to "more deeply understand where weird fiction came from—and where it might go"?

DP: Before I start I should make a quick addendum to the previous answer. I've just discovered that Sheffield City Archives have some of Gilchrist's diaries, albeit from the later years of his life. These aren't digitized or even indexed, so they're only available in person at the archives; I've asked for an appointment to see them at some point in the (hopefully near) future. I believe that they basically have a box of his papers that were donated some years ago, but they've not been investigated thoroughly. It'll be interesting to see what they hold!

For me, *The Stone Dragon* is important because it sits at a nexus of distinct but interlinked literary genres. Gilchrist was born in the same year that Baudelaire died and Gilchrist himself died in the same year that Lovecraft wrote "The Tomb" (although it would be several years before the story was published). This bookends Gilchrist with Decadence at one end and the weird at the other. Also, *The Stone Dragon* was published only a few years before Stoker's *Dracula*. The tales in *The Stone Dragon* blend the florid, cloying scents of Decadence (often literally as Gilchrist repeatedly uses flowers and plants, like honeysuckle or yarrow, as motifs in his stories) with the decay and haunted legacies of the Gothic, whilst simultaneously looking forward to what would become weird fiction. I think it's this breadth of horror that makes *The Stone Dragon* such an important work, especially when you expand it with tales such as "The Crimson Weaver" or "The Holocaust," which were published elsewhere. "The Basilisk" has a different tone to "My Friend," which has a different tone to "The Manuscript of Francis Shackerley," but they all work together and obviously spring from the same source. Even a story such as "The Return," which is at face value a fairly simple ghost story, has layers of meaning hidden within for those who wish to look for them. I think this is also reflected in the amount of literary voices Gilchrist had; even ignoring the different themes and narratives of his weirder fiction, he also wrote his "Peak" tales in a Derbyshire dialect and his novels in a much more formal manner.

What it meant for Gilchrist is harder to imagine. Personally, I think he wrote novels as a way to gain some legitimacy in critical circles, but it's short fiction that he was truly enthusiastic about. Gilchrist often runs out of steam in his longer works and they drag on a bit longer than they should, but he's never afraid of ending a short work exactly when it needs to. Walpole tells us that Gilchrist "died, in the first years of the War, a disappointed but never embittered man." I get the feeling, albeit largely unsubstantiated, that this disappointment comes more from the lackluster reception of *The Stone Dragon* more than any other of his writings. I might be able to get a better feel for that if I can get access to the diaries in the Sheffield Archive.

AH: That's pretty exciting! Can't wait to read about what you may find.

Speaking of the breadth and interlinking genres of Gilchrist's short stories, you have divided the collection into four distinct parts. While you introduce these sections in the collection itself, can you explain for our readers how you have chosen to arrange *I Am Stone* and what sort of arc this may create for the collection as a whole? Additionally, while I think you are right that many of these stories have very distinct tones from one another, they are also all unmistakably Gilchrist. To you, what does it mean to be a Gilchrist story? There will almost certainly be an abundance of flower and plant motifs but what else may be at work?

DP: The division into sections came about for a number of reasons. The most prosaic was that I wanted to provide some contextual header notes for the stories and to add this into the main introduction just seemed too unwieldy. Breaking the stories into thematic sections, each with their own mini-introduction, was the natural way to approach it. I did also want to highlight some of the major themes of Gilchrist's stories, and grouping certain stories together helped with that. The Peak stories were the most obvious as they stand slightly apart from Gilchrest's other works from the start in their heavy use of local dialect. After that, I tried to use what I think of as Gilchrist's major motifs as a guide. Firstly we have Gilchrist's fascination with beings who may not be undead but are unliving. Many of Gilchrist's stories feature characters who are not-quite-alive to varying degrees, from the ghostly Rose of "The Return" to the strange distance of Phyllida from "Midsummer Madness." I think this speaks to Gilchrist's love of times past and how they linger on in the present. We also have the repeated presence of male protagonists who are listless and ineffectual; "useless heroes," as Gilchrist calls them. This is probably most evident in "The Basilisk," where we get the distinct impression that the (male) narrator is being taken advantage of by the (female) subject of the story. I find it really interesting how pretty much all of Gilchrist's stories are narrated by men, but he uses this to show how men can be distracted from the real events or even, sometimes, just downright thick. Finally we have Gilchrist's obsession with "passion." We probably think of passion nowadays as meaning fervent, heated love, but Gilchrist is using it in the more precise form of suffering, and the endurance of that suffering (the most immediate examples of this are the passions of the martyrs and of Christ). For Gilchrist, love and suffering and death are all bound tightly together, and this is no doubt tied to the way in which his sexuality would have forced him to live his life in a very restricted, confined way. I think these categories do form an arc in Gilchrist's writing with a sense of not being fully in the world, a frustration and disappointment with what it is to be a man and then a mournful sense of struggle and pain.

As for the anatomy of a Gilchrist story, there are certainly some other repeating ideas. Flower motifs and symbology are ever-present, but so is the natural world in animals and even landscape. Gilchrist continually uses the north of England, most often Derbyshire but also Lancashire and Cumbria, as the setting of his stories, with his Peak tales being immersed in the local area. There's also often a deeply archaic, even anachronistic, sense to his writing, with people and artworks of the seventeenth and eighteenth centuries being invoked almost as asides but used to add layers to the narrative, like the brief but pointed mention of Robert Herrick in "The Writings of Althea Swarthmoor." Perhaps more subtly, I think Gilchrist manages to take what are often quite abrupt stories—most of them are very short and most of them end in quite a rapid manner—but imbue them with a depth, a kind of richness. There's a feeling, for me at least, that the stories persist and intertwine with one another outside of the evident narrative.

AH: You have touched upon them quite a bit in your prior answer, but I wonder if you wouldn't mind elaborating a little more on the Peak stories.

I found myself charmed by those that are included in this collection as well as being somewhat surprised. My introduction to and knowledge of Gilchrist were framed in his status as a forerunner to weird fiction; and yet, as you mention in the introduction, and as I discovered reading some articles about him in the lead-up to this discussion, his reputation appears to have been greatly bolstered by the Peak tales. At the time of his death the *Derbyshire Courier* referred to Gilchrist as "The Peak Novelist," and you include in the section introduction a 1951 line from the *Derbyshire Countryside* describing them as "real as Derbyshire oat-cake and sage-cheese." While the three stories included do, as you put it, "maintain a weird glimmer," that appears to be the exception rather than the rule for the

Peak tales as a whole. However, when I looked up a few others online, they were still rather unmistakably Gilchrist.

I suppose, if I have to frame it as a question, I wonder if it is really necessary, or fair, to keep the Peak tales separate from the more "traditionally" Gothic tales of Gilchrist? The Peak tales do not seem as if they were something Gilchrist was writing merely to pay the bills or win popularity . . . How do you personally view them?

DP: I think Gilchrist genuinely loved writing his Peak tales and he certainly wrote a lot of them, no doubt because the inspiration for them was right on his doorstop. He was a perennial rambler—enjoying what Walpole describes as "a long moorland tramp"—so no doubt came across scenes and people who could be built into stories. He also wrote nonfiction guidebooks and gazetteers to the area, so I think there's more of an interest in the place in itself than there is in simply siphoning off inspiration. There is a bit of a double-edged sword here, however, as London was the center of publishing and, then as now, London always focuses on regionality. I think that the picturesque nature of many of Gilchrist's stories appealed to London audiences as a quaint diversion more than the social commentary that Gilchrist might have wanted them to be. This is perhaps too cynical, though, as a feature in the *Idler* (printed in Volume 29 of its half-yearly collections) states that "in his studies of the present-day life of peakland folk, Mr Gilchrist appeals as a master of the short story [. . .] He does not, let it be understood, paint the landscape in on a big scale, with many details—rather the reverse. He puts the human interest first, and creates the scenic background after the manner of the delicate etcher."

I do think, certainly, that there is a Gothic sensibility to the Peak tales, largely due to their setting but also the adversity faced by the characters. *The Strolling Player* is one of Gilchrist's gloomiest novels and yet nothing supernatural is even hinted at; it is the poverty of the characters and the harshness of the landscape in which they suffer that poverty that causes the gloom. There's something inherently Gothic about moors and windswept hillsides, with their blasted trees and silent marshes. I'm sure that Gilchrist would have been very aware of novels such as *Wuthering Heights* and *Jane Eyre,* written by the Brontës in their own Gothic landscape of the Yorkshire Dales just on the other side of Leeds from Gilchrist's Peak District. I'm sure more of his Peak tales definitely could be folded into the more overtly Gothic tales, and that's something I want to work on in the future.

AH: I am glad you mentioned the prevalence of adversity in the Peak tales, as adversity appears to me to be one of the defining characteristics of a Gilchrist tale.

You have previously discussed the major motifs of Gilchrist's work and how each section reflects them, and I feel that the overarching theme and the thread that binds the collection together is adversity. In particular, it is an unknown or unclear struggle, simply a state the characters find themselves in, and a lot of the horror or weirdness of the tales seems intertwined with the foreboding sense of failing to overcome such abstract challenges. There are Gilchrist's "useless heroes" as you put it—and I am hard pressed to think of a more useless hero than the narrator of "Witch In-Grain"—but it goes beyond characters failing to rise to the heroic occasion: it's characters simply drowning in what the world demands of them. The narrator of "The Crimson Weaver" wishes to save his master but seems to have little idea what is actually plaguing his master and how to help, and so he has to bear witness to . . . something . . .

Does this reading of Gilchrist make sense? Is it fair to say that struggle is a key component of Gilchrist's work? If not, how might you frame it?

DP: I think adversity and struggle are big parts of Gilchrist's work, yes. The forces that his characters encounter are often shadowy and ill-defined, but I think this is less because of Gilchrist's failings as a writer and more an intentional attempt to show these struggles as happening in an uncertain world, for uncertain ends. There's a collapse of expectation of "how things should be," which I think cuts to the heart of horror in general and weird horror in particular. I think there's also something to be said for this feeling simply being part of Gilchrist's character. I'm also from Northern England, albeit from the other side of Manchester from Gilchrist's haunts, and we have a rather gloomy tendency to expect adversity (even to the extent of inventing it when it doesn't appear). There are lots of reasons for this; the weather tends to be damp and cold, the work has tended to be industrial and poorly paid, and there's a general stubbornness of character. People from the North of England often feel that their lives are dominated by forces outside of their influence and comprehension—London-centric politics, the invisible hand of capitalism—and the belief that an honest day's work should receive an honest day's pay is often undermined by the workings of these forces.

However, I do think there's a deeper reason for this sense of "drowning in what the world demands of them," as you put it, and that relates to Gilchrist's experiences as a gay man. The Victorian attitude to homosexuality was far more complicated than the common view that it was universally abhorred, but any sense of acceptance or safety would more than likely exist in the cities, especially London. Provincial attitudes in the North of England, even today, are less tolerant. The sense of embattlement and even bewilderment at a world that appears to dish out punishment for no apparent reason makes a lot of sense when you understand that Gilchrist probably felt embattled just for being himself. There's a bit of an ironic twist in this, too, as Gilchrist probably would have found more acceptance if he'd conformed to the opposite stereotype of an outgoing, decadent figure when, in fact, he supported temperance causes and enjoyed bracing walks in the countryside far more than the smogs of London.

I definitely think that the idea of struggling with a world that seems not to have a place for you and Gilchrist's persistent theme of passion as a source of suffering because of love, in its widest sense, are key to his work.

AH: At the risk of having you do my job for me, are there any other aspects of Gilchrist's work that we have not touched upon that you would like to mention? You have cited a few stories in our discussion . . . if this conversation were to be readers' first introduction to Robert Murray Gilchrist, where would you recommend they start? I mean, obviously, I would say they should read *I Am Stone* in its entirety, but let's say they only have time for a few stories to get to know Gilchrist's work.

DP: I would start where I started, with "The Crimson Weaver." If that doesn't capture your imagination and draw you in then his other work might be a hard sell. After that I'd suggest "The Return," which is a good insight into how Gilchrist uses insinuation and implication to drive his narratives. Happily, both of these (along with my introduction) can be read for free by using the Look Inside feature on the book's Amazon page (shorturl.at/jnEG9).

I think we've covered the main aspects of Gilchrist's weird fiction, at least. His novel-length romances are something I want to try and explore more, but they're so hard to get hold of. One thing that is perhaps worth stressing is that, as far as I can see, he seems to have been universally liked and considered to be a fundamentally decent person. In an obituary the writer Eden Phillpotts notes Gilchrist's "tolerance and genial, humour-lighted outlook on existence," and his funeral was attended not just by friends and family but, as the *Derbyshire Courier* of the time tells us, "the Belgian refugees [from World War I] billeted nearby to whom Mr Gilchrist had shown great kindness." There's a slight sadness to think that Gilchrist's lack of success in his time and his rapid fade from public awareness may well have stemmed, at least in part, from simply being too nice.

AH: Well, now there is something I should really try to model my life around: being so nice that I am simply forgotten after death. Joking aside, thanks to work like yours, I am glad to see Gilchrist receiving some of the attention and critical success his work merits.

Aside from reviewing the Sheffield City Archives, do you see more Gilchrist-related work in your future? If not Gilchrist, are there other projects you are currently working on that you are at liberty to share? Where can readers find more of your work outside of our very own journal?

DP: I've rather tentatively started thinking about a biography of Gilchrist, which would rely on the documents in the Sheffield Archive and other resources like the letters of William Sharp, a friend of Gilchrist's. I'm always looking out for mention of other weird tales; I'm not sure that anybody knew that "The Holocaust" existed, for example, so it's not too far-fetched to hope that there may be more. I'd also like to look more deeply into the Peak tales.

My main focus at the moment is catching up on some of my review commitments. I've just submitted reviews for Gina Wisker's excellent *Contemporary Women's Gothic Fiction* and the Devil's Advocate companion to *The Witch*. I'm also planning a new lecture for the Romancing the Gothic project on Haunted Houses in Video Games, which should be a lot of fun. After that, my next project is a chapter for the Palgrave *Handbook of the Vampire,* where I'll be looking at the vampires of Speculative Horror. My blog—pietersender.wordpress.com—is probably the best place to keep up to date with the articles and lectures that I work on. Everything ends up on there eventually!

AH: Wonderful stuff all around—I am very excited to hear what the Sheffield Archive may hold! As we wrap up, I am curious, what are you currently reading for fun?

DP: I'm currently reading the Alien trilogy novelisation by Alan Dean Foster and the rulebook for the new version of the Kill Team skirmish wargame!

AH: Hah, I imagine the trilogy must be fun and I wish you the best of luck with the rulebook!

Thank you very much for taking the time to discuss Gilchrist. I am most grateful this has not ended with either of us half-dead watching hour by hour the bloody clew ever unwinding from our heart—or, at least, I hope that is not the state you are in.

DP: I am, as ever, completely clew-less . . .

It's been a lot of fun. Thanks for the interesting and thoughtful questions!

Cheers.

The Friend, the Romances, and the Revelation

The joey Zone

R. MURRAY GILCHRIST. *I Am Stone: The Gothic Weird Tales*. Edited by Daniel Pietersen. London: British Library, 2021. 320 pp. £8.99 tpb. ISBN: 9780712354004.

1.

> I walked in pain, as though giant spiders had woven about my body. On the terrace strange beasts—dogs and pigs with human limbs—tore ravenously at something that lay beside the balustrade . . . the monsters dispersed hurriedly among the dropping blossoms of the pleasaunce, and where they had swarmed I saw naught but a steaming sanguine pool . . .

Not in Kadath, nor a Hodgsonian nightmare, we are in equally dark dreamlands here.

Tragical romances as stylistically rich as those of Robert Murray Gilchrist (1867–1917), like old acquaintances, ought not be forgotten and always brought to print. The British Library Tales of the Weird series and *Dead Reckonings* contributor Daniel Pietersen raise a cup of kindness to share with us all.

In 1975, Hugh Lamb's *Terror by Gaslight* reprinted Gilchrist's "The Basilisk." Other selections followed in further anthologies by Lamb. Collections of the writer have unfortunately been out of print for more than a decade. *A Night on the Moor,* the Wordsworth paperback edition, and the earlier Ash-Tree Press hardcover, *The Basilisk and Other Tales of Dread* (2003), contained the bulk of the material in this present volume. The latter's cover by Ash-Tree stalwart Paul Lowe is gorgeous (well, to those of us with predilection for venomous mythopoeic taxonomies) but somewhat misleading to its contents overall. Lowe's painting for Frances Oliver's *Dancing on Air* (Ash-Tree Press, 2004) could rather more accurately represent one of Gilchrist's tales, for example.

Two women artists lend a truer feel to this current imprint, which will hopefully have a lengthier availability. *I Am Stone* cover artist Sandra Gómez also contributes a frontispiece sharing a time-warped synchronicity with the plate "St. George" by the occult artist W. T. Horton (*The Book of Images,* 1898). Photography by Fay Godwin introduces each section of the tales, perfectly documenting the genius loci of Gilchrist's moody Peak District. In one case, there is evidence of what appears to be a basilisk skeleton . . .

2.

Among more than a half dozen scholarly essays Pietersen has written about Gilchrist in this journal before: "Bestarred with Fainting Flowers: Symbolism and Myth in the Work of R. Murray Gilchrist" (*Dead Reckonings* No. 21) and "I No longer Live in This House: The Liminality of Undeath in the Works of R. Murray Gilchrist" (*Dead Reckonings* No. 26).

Pietersen postulates that Gilchrist is a *liminal* writer, that is, his work falls through the cracks between Gothic, Decadent, and weird genres. It would be a mistake to adhere to the writings of the author any of these labels, albeit a majority of the stories here are Gothic in tone. The Decadent category, let alone weird, can only truly apply to a handful of Gilchrist's more ornate fictions, including the aforementioned "Basilisk" and "The Crimson Weaver." One might classify some other stories as folk horror, such as "The Panicle" and the greatest revelation in this volume, "My Friend."

All labels aside, Gilchrist's writing sets an alluring bejeweled snare for the reader's interest despite the frameworks of melodrama in these narratives. The *Spectator* said of Gilchrist's writing in his first novel *Passion and Plaything* (1890) that it was "an unpleasant book, containing far too much in the way of sensuous description." We will always assent to more of *that,* please. Several stories of his do have abrupt endings ("The Stone Dragon"), sometimes not quite clear in their resolution à la Frank Stockton.

In some of his later writing, however, Gilchrist developed a clearer, more direct style that does add to the telling. The tragic "The Madness of Betty Hooton" and the darkly comic "Sir

Toby's Wife" (which Pietersen dug up for this collection from the British Library vaults) are examples. The giggling sexton in the second tale could have been a role for that splendid ham barnstormer of the last century, Tod Slaughter.

Pietersen ascribes greater agency to Gilchrist's female characters as opposed to the ofttimes weak, passive male narrators. But this may be just wishful thinking. Female antagonists such as "The Crimson Weaver" fall easily into the fin de siècle trope of La Belle Dame Sans Merci:

> Stooping, with sidelong motions of the head, she approached: bringing with her the smell of such an incense as when amidst Eastern herbs burns the corpse . . . She was perfect as the Diana, but her skin was deathly white . . .

The protagonist Marina in "The Basilisk" is no less objectified:

> Her beauty . . . was pale and reposeful, the loveliness of a marble image . . . I had found her laden with flaming tendrils in the thinned woods of my heritage. A very Dryad, robed in grass colour, she was chanting to the sylvan deities. The invisible web took me, and I became her slave.

3.

Gilchrist wrote twenty-two novels, six short story collections, and four regional guidebooks. He must have been somewhat successful, but who was he writing for? Gilchrist was something of a country dandy, who periodically appeared in his local parish wearing a cassock and girdle (predating Montague Summers stylistically). Existing photos of him show a sweaty tousle-headed Scot with physiognomy of a Highland Jean Lorrain; on closer inspection a sly gleam betrayed in the eye of the author posing as Decadent.

Gilchrist's apprenticeship to the cutlery business until he was twenty-one might have been where he met George Alfred Garfill, who worked in his own family's scythe works. *The Stone Dragon and Other Tragical Romances* was dedicated to Garfill, who would be Robert's companion from 1895 until his death.

"My Friend" might be the one story especially written for George. And himself: "the friend I had won (the first and the last) loved me so dearly that he would be unhappy unless his hand were clasping mine . . ." Parts of this story reads like actual biographical entry:

> Circumstances had bound him to a profession that chafed his very core: but Nature had given him aspirations, and miraged him a future as great (if as worthless) as my own. How daring I grew! Farther and farther I had ventured down the heretical abyss.

The narrator and his friend journey to the countryside and come to a set of Druid stones. What follows is—a meditation? Or is it a flashback to an ancestral memory?

> A sacrificial hymn was beginning at the Circle—a naked and bleeding victim was bound to the altar . . . the long bearded priests shook their white robes—the sharp knife glittered—and my own stiletto waxed heavy, as it strove to draw me downwards . . . Again the skies opened, but with only a momentary gleam; one glance of the Almighty Eye. But it was not so swift as to prevent me from seeing the face of the Sacrifice.

"My Friend" is worth the cost of admission to this ceremony and this volume alone.

4.

Pietersen states that there are a mere eight copies of Gilchrist's novel *The Labyrinth* (1902) on public loan to the entire world. The *Spectator* review of it upon release—"a book with an atmosphere of nightmare"—whets one's interest. "The characters, mostly bizarre and some repellent" include "a witch . . . a baggage of a girl . . . the profligate fine-gentleman hero of the story . . . a leper . . . It is all fantastic beyond description, but the morbid extravagance of the plot is in a measure redeemed by the skill of the literary treatment." Friend and critic Arnold Bennett said:

> Murray Gilchrist's best work lies in his short stories, some of which are merely and quite simply perfect . . . [but] *The Labyrinth* . . . is astounding. *The Labyrinth* is like a rich, mellow naïve eighteenth century tapestry; whenever I think of it,

I think of it as the one truly original modern English novel . . . Perhaps in about twenty years it will be the correct thing to have read him. ["Books and Persons," *New Age* (21 March 1908): 412]

A humble plea then.

After immersing ourselves in the language (a fourteen page "Notes on the Text" with glossary is included with the archaic seventeenth-century terms and references Gilchrist used in his stories) and revelations of *I Am Stone,* we need a reprint now of this—possibly tragic?—romance of the House of the Eleven Staircases. With, of course, no one less than Daniel Pietersen at the helm editorially, brought to print by *some* canny independent publisher . . .

After more than one hundred years it would be the correct thing.

Alice Through the Witching Glass

Oliver Sheppard

The House That Eats the Rabbit. Cosmotropia de Xam, dir. 2021. Phantasma Disques.

In the preface to his groundbreaking 1896 anthology of Symbolist prose and poetry, *The Book of Masks,* French writer Remy de Gourmont rhetorically asked:

> What is Symbolism? Practically nothing, if we adhere to the narrow etymological sense. If we pass beyond, it may mean individualism in literature, liberty in art, abandonment of taught formulas, tendencies toward the new and strange, or even towards the bizarre. It may also mean idealism, a contempt for the social anecdote, anti-naturalism, a propensity to seize only the characteristic details of life, to emphasize only those acts that distinguish one man from another, to strive to achieve essentials; and finally, for the poets, symbolism seems allied to free verse, that is, to unswathed verse whose young body may frolic at ease, liberated from embarrassments of swaddling clothes and straps.

These thoughts from Remy de Gourmont are more than 120 years old. That is, they are not exactly any part of a cutting-edge sentiment; and de Gourmont's nineteenth-century observations are perhaps even, by now, traditional or even conventional thought, if 120+ years' passage of time can allow something to be admitted into the canon of "tradition." Cosmotropia de Xam's newest film, *The House That Eats the Rabbit,* which was quickly filmed over five days in 2021 during the recent pandemic lockdown in Europe, might as well have taken de Gourmont's thoughts as its guidance. As with most of Cosmotropia de Xam's films, this movie flaunts conventions of narrative and theme, and is a darkly impressionistic visual affair.

The House That Eats the Rabbit is a surreal, underground, arthouse film that traffics in the general ambiance of 1970s

European Gothic-surrealist cinema, a form of cinema that seemed (especially in the hands of 1970s filmmakers such as Jean Rollin and even Andy Warhol) to take to heart de Gourmont's thoughts relayed above. At its root, the film serves as a dreamlike meditation upon Lewis Carroll's *Alice's Adventures in Wonderland* as well as its sequel, *Through the Looking Glass.* Indeed, every one of de Xam's more than fifteen movies are probably best described as modern, low-budget, arthouse, Gothic, psychedelic, visual tone poems that evince a strong affinity for cult, underground European horror and experimental filmmaking from the past fifty years. The connection between de Xam's filmography and vintage cult Eurocinema was brought into stark relief by the recent major distribution deal offered to Cosmotropia de Xam by Nigel Wingrove's Salvation and Redemption Films label in the UK, a major distributor of "Euro-sploitation" cult cinema that includes the films of Jess Franco, Lucio Fulci, and Jean Rollin.

For those encountering this director for the first time, "Cosmotropia de Xam" is obviously a pseudonym. De Xam himself is a shadowy moviemaker who's a) definitely European and b) almost certainly German. (English- and German-language versions of *The House That Eats the Rabbit* exist, but even the English-language version of this movie—which clocks in at about 66 minutes in length—contains English narration delivered with a thick German accent.) De Xam's last name refers to the late 1960s psychedelic graphic novel *Saga de Xam,* a comic written by French Euro-exploitation director Jean Rollin, and which is about a blue-skinned girl from the planet Xam. Rollin directed many Gothic-surrealist vampire movies in the late 1960s and 1970s, and those movies serve as a major visual touchstone for *The House That Eats the Rabbit.*

Indeed, there's a clue at the beginning of the film as the opening credits roll: it is announced that it is based on a book by "Sue R. Lism." Serving as a kind a pun on the word "surrealism," Ms. Sue R. Lism has indeed been behind a lot of de Xam's filmography, and in rare interviews the mysterious de Xam has indeed described himself as a surrealist filmmaker.

Take these surrealist and Euro-horror reference points as a hint here, if not an outright warning: if you need your films to have conventional narrative structures, clearly defined protagonists and antagonists, and if you need your movies to have no attendant ambiguity in theme or meaning—and, as well, if you need your films to look as if they've been bankrolled by deep pockets at major Hollywood studios, slick and made for mass audiences—then the films of Cosmotropia de Xam are definitely not for you. The DIY ethos is in full effect. *The House That Eats the Rabbit* belongs to a revival of a tradition of '60s and '70s Euro-surrealist-cum-exploitation filmmaking that does have some vogue now, but here it is done on the cheap and with obvious digital filters applied in post-production, like the "glitchy," film-like artifacts that have obviously been applied to the raw digital video of this movie, in post, to give *The House That Eats the Rabbit* an artificially vintage look.

The costumes in the film also harken to the days of the 1970s: the primary actresses wear flowery (and, frankly, gorgeous) gowns that seem to recall, in a strange way, the wardrobes of maidens in pre-Raphaelite paintings. And as with the films of Jean Rollin in the 1970s, most of the central drivers of the story of the movie are attractive women in their twenties or thirties. (The filmic universe of Cosmotropia de Xam in fact normally admits men only in cameos or in very rare, limited, special appearances.) De Xam has admitted in interviews that the films of Jess Franco and Jean Rollin have acted as his chief artistic lodestars; and those directors, too, preferred attractive women in main roles—if not most roles, whether main or secondary.

So how does *The House That Eats the Rabbit* take on the storylines of Lewis Carroll? Obliquely and laterally, is the answer. Diagonally. Impressionistically.

First of all, there exists a curious dichotomy regarding the dramatis personae of the *The House That Eats the Rabbit:* in this film, Lewis Carroll's famous character, Alice, is bifurcated into a "White Alice" (played by Mira Kohli) and a "Black Alice" (played by Marijana Mladenov). The "White Alice" wears a white robe and the "Black Alice" wears a black robe. (Both are white European women, incidentally.) Conversely, two other famous characters from Lewis Carroll's Wonderland universe, the White Rabbit and the Mad Hatter, are here collapsed into a single entity, played admirably by Adriani Schmidt; and she is probably the best actor in this film.

What narrative there is to speak of throughout the film is vague. "I would recommend people watch this movie from a metaphysical perspective," Cosmotropia de Xam told the *Escapist Advisor* blog recently. (Note: Gene Willow's blog serves as an important source of information about Cosmotropia de Xam; and "Gene Willow" is also almost certainly a pseudonym, too, as Willow claims he is a Ukrainian blogger, probably of Germanic extraction.) This is a symbolic and not a literal movie.

The main character of *The House That Eats the Rabbit* is not a human being at all; it is, rather, the house itself, which is alluded to in the movie's title. Locale, ambiance, and atmosphere are generally more important "characters" in the films of Cosmotropia de Xam than the flesh-and-blood characters played by human actors. De Xam stated that the setting of the house in *The House That Eats the Rabbit,* which was built in 1900, was a major character. And de Xam had wondered how many dreamlike tales the house itself had witnessed, if it had had a sense of perception. How does a house perceive time and what "memories" does it hold within its walls?

It is worth noting that works of one of the most "European" of American auteurs, David Lynch, also figures large in the makeup of this movie. Weighing heavily upon the mood of *The House That Eats the Rabbit* are Lynch's *Twin Peaks* series (and especially its *Fire Walk with Me* prequel movie and the most recent "third season" of *Twin Peaks,* which pushed the limits of surrealist entertainment on Showtime)—and the 2006 digital movie *Inland Empire.* Lynch's digital experimentation this century has given a green light, of sorts, for modern underground directors to work in a digital, iPhone-driven, low-budget milieu.

The modernist poet Wallace Stevens said, "A poem need not have a meaning and like most things in nature often does not have." This is really a paraphrase of Charles Baudelaire's famous mid-nineteenth-century sentiment that "A poem need not mean anything; it only needs to be something." Similarly,

Cosmotropia de Xam's films do not "mean"; they "are." There is a certain school of film (and literary) criticism that wants to find a Rosetta Stone to interpret obviously abstract works so that, with that interpretative cipher in hand, such seemingly obscure works suddenly "make sense" and follow a logical order. But that is beside the point. There is no way that dream-like meditations upon literary works—meditations upon dreams—upon life itself—need to "make sense" in any certain, teleological way. That is a poor, vulgar, and limiting understanding of the bounds of human imagination and art, which is the attendant consequence of human imagination. Cosmotropia de Xam's *The House That Eats the Rabbit* deserves to be taken on its own terms—as a darkly surreal, impressionistic, neo-Gothic experiment in modern filmmaking.

Cosmotropia de Xam is also the founder of the witch-house music collective Mater de Suspiria Vision. Not to be confused with Evangeline Walton's *Witch House* novel from the 1940s, published by Arkham House, modern witch-house music began this century, and de Xam's group provides the lulling, dreamy soundtrack to *The House That Eats the Rabbit,* available on de Xam's Phantasma Disques label. (phantasmadisques.bigcartel.com/)

Our Last Gasp—"Good Lord! *Choke* It's Eco-Horror!"

The joey Zone

JON B. COOKE and RONALD E. TURNER. *Slow Death Zero*. San Francisco, CA: Last Gasp, 2020. 128 pp. $24.95 tpb. ISBN: 9780867198836.

> I called the doctor
> Up in the morning
> I had a fever
> It was a warning
> She said "There's nothing I can prescribe
> To keep your raunchy bag of bones alive"
> I got some money left for one more shot
> She said "God bless you" I said "Thanks a lot"
> It's a slow, slow death.
>
> —The Flaming Groovies, "Slow Death" (1972)

San Francisco's proto-punks The Flaming Groovies' lyrics refer to an unrepentant addiction. It was a warning THEN. If you've smelled the Purple Haze in the skies from out-of-control wildfires or had a Hard Rain fall by the feet in the NOW of 2021, it could also refer to humanity's current self-injected climate catastrophe(s).

As a Hippocampus reader, why should YOU be interested?

Contributors Richard Corben, Cody Goodfellow, Mike Dubisch, Skinner, and the initiator of this all-new fiftieth anniversary collection, Jon B. Cooke, have all done their servitude in the Lovecraftian art and literary mines. But there is a different grade of ore here.

Cooke pens a six-page history of *Slow Death,* which inaugurated two years before that Flaming Groovies single—it would be reason enough to pick up this anthology alone. As he has done with in-depth articles for *Comic Book Artist* (TwoMorrows Publishing), Jon serves up a thorough look at the underground comic title, What It Is and How It Came to Be, with every cover of the original run reproduced. Gary Arlington, who started the San Francisco Comic Book Company that published it, had a vision: "My dream is for E. C. Comics [the groundbreaking 1950s publishers of *Weird Science, Two-Fisted Tales,* among other titles] to return with the better underground cartoonists." Ron Turner was another fan. Drew Friedman contributes an inside front cover portrait of "Baba" Ron, The Once and Future founder and Last Gasp guru and this publication's co-editor. Ken Meyer Jr.'s vignette of Cooke in Wally Wood-ish space gear should be a T-shirt design for us fans (some of us dating from JBC's seminal '90s fanzine *Tekeli-li!*). Make it so.

From the thirty artists and accompanying six writers here are a few highlights then, reflecting toxic rainbows:

William Stout's art will always get this writer's attention. A great cover showcasing his rich detailed style is followed by a 7-page piece that is more optimistic than most of its company called "Antarctica". He states:

> The world's greatest photographers all noted that it was impossible to capture the *color* of the continent because of color photography's chemical limitations . . . as an *artist*, I don't have that limitation—whatever colors I see I can put down onto paper!

The Colour out of Antarctica, indeed. Stout had done three covers in a row for the original run of *Slow Death,* the "Two-Fisted" homage on #8's Greenpeace Issue being a standout and predecessor to this current collection.

Richard Corben is responsible for possibly the best comic—excuse me—graphic narrative adaptation of H. P. Lovecraft ever done, "The Rats in the Walls" (*Skull* #5, 1972). One of the last pieces done before his recent passing, "Garbage Man" is included here, in contrast to Stout's storyline being one of the bleakest. "With a nod & thanks to Richard Corben & Howie" ("When Howie Made It in the Real World," *Slow Death* #2, 1972), Jon Cooke notes in the Errol McCarthy–illustrated tale "Last Chance Gas" that he penned. It has a happy (?) if not righteous ending for its two protagonists.

Richard Corben serves up his usual tasty fare. It is an honor to include "Gore" in a Hippocampus publication. © Bruce Jones and estate of Richard Corben

Cody Goodfellow and Mike Dubisch (*Black Velvet Cthulhu*) team up for two offerings, "Flotsam & Jetsam" and "Terminal Colony." Both are scathing indictments of those who become part of the solution only to become a bigger problem. Spoiler: the cancer on the Earth may be US. Goodfellow in particular has proven a true discerning conscience for the enlightened weird community but is no Cody Comelately. We are lucky to have him visit this planet.

A Wizard, A True Star, the Bay Area's Skinner delivers a Panter-esque double page spread of E.C.-like aliens finding our world already trashed: "But hey! At least the flooding makes for some good tubin' across town!" says greeter Baba Ron, trying to scam some beers.

Brooklyn's Danny Hellman (whom I first encountered by covers done for the fanzine *Brutarian*) ends the book with a faux comic book cover for *The Fighting Hippie* #18, with Ron Turner breaking that fourth wall to save penguin hugger Greta Thunberg (to whom this whole book is dedicated) from the evil machinations of John D. Rockefeller. There is a suggestion by Jon Cooke of future issues beyond this celebratory revival.

If we make it that long of course before our last gasp.

Slow death . . . eat my mind away
Slow death . . . turn my guts to clay
Slow death
Yeah, yeah.

The Dead Worth Waking

Karen Joan Kohoutek

BRETT RUTHERFORD, ed. *Wake Not the Dead! Continental Tales of Terror*. Pittsburgh, PA: Grim Reaper Books, 2021. 200 pp. $18.95 tpb. ISBN: 9798734684313.

Discovering new, obscure nineteenth-century Gothic writers in 2021, in a form edited and typeset for the convenience of modern readers, is like discovering a dusty coffin in the ruins of an ancient church and finding a perfectly preserved body inside, its cheeks flushed and lips red with fresh blood. In a word: delightful! That's what I found in the anthology *Wake Not the Dead! Continental Tales of Terror*. Brett Rutherford has edited and adapted works from 1823 to 1876, by Germans Ernst Raupach and Ludwig Tieck (including a story that inspired Richard Wagner's famous opera *Tannhäuser*), and writing partners Émile Erckmann and Alexandre Chatrian, from Lorraine, who wrote in French, despite the region's predominant use of German.

While German writings had a prominent place in the origins of the Romantic movement and the associated popularity of the Gothic, many are unavailable in English translations, apart from scans from early books which can feel off-puttingly antiquarian for everyday reading. Rutherford's process has, by his own account in the introduction, involved "modernizing the language and embellishing considerably." Some of the adaptations are small, and others, as in Tieck's "And Never to Part," are substantial; Rutherford details the changes, so the reader can know which elements are original and which are new additions. A detailed bibliography is also included, for those who want to explore the writers beyond these adapted versions.

The bulk of the collection is made up of Tieck's work, with only two stories by Erckmann-Chatrian and one from Raupach. However, Raupach's piece is featured prominently as the first in the book, as well as providing the title: "Wake Not the Dead!" In this tale, a grief-stricken husband, Walter, mourns "as though the dead and their ghosts could hear him, under the tall linden trees by her mausoleum, while his head reclined on the cold stone of a nameless grave," immediately steeping us in classic Gothic atmosphere. When a sorcerer helps him bring his dead first wife back from the grave to teach him a lesson, an evil is unleashed with dire consequences for all, since "her capacity to feed was infinite; it could go on until she herself should, at the Last Day, be consumed with the earth itself!"

The vampiric first wife is named Brunhilda, and the second wife Swanhilda. These names from northern European mythology give the story the feeling of a folktale, even as the situation grows increasingly Poe-like, a similarity Rutherford says he played up in his version.

A strong theme in Raupach's tale is how the desire for the ideal can sour appreciation of the real. While Brunhilda was difficult in life, Walter puts her memory on a pedestal after her death, an act that poisons his second marriage, destroys his relationship with his children, and ultimately condemns him. The gentle Swanhilda tries to steer her passionate husband's "aspirations after unattainable enjoyments, to the duties and pleasures of actual life," but Brunhilda puts her victims under a spell of pleasure and luxury: "They were the most anxious for that which was to prove their destruction; yet do we not all aspire after that which conducts us to the grave—after the enjoyment of life? These innocents stretched out their arms to approaching death because it assumed the mask of pleasure."

This theme is also prominent in the majority of Tieck's tales, which contain Gothic tropes like castles, crypts, and descriptions of landscapes that mirror emotional states, along with ideas from literary Romanticism, which are not treated uncritically but sometimes critiqued. For example, one of the stories about excursions to fairyland, "The Elves," addresses why people are so drawn to stories of the ideal and unchanging. A little girl is irresistibly attracted to the beauties of a fantasy world as an explicit contrast to everyday life, which is described as "so pained by the transitory nature of life and beauty." This story also reflects the tendency of people to center their own importance and misunderstand the complicated cause and effect of the world.

In "And Never to Part," about a man who strays into a different fairyland where "every conscious and unconscious wish was satisfied," the supernatural realm is seductive, a place of sexual experimentation, but also potentially threatening, cutting him off from the rest of humanity. Similarly, "Tannenhaüser" deals with a visitor to a dreamland populated by pagan gods and mythical beings, drawn in but ultimately wearied by it. "The Price of Love," which would make a good, ironic horror movie, openly mocks the main character, a Romantic figure for whom "everything must be in the superlative . . . Everything must be pure, and majestic, and ethereal, and celestial. His heart must be always throbbing and heaving, even when he is standing before a puppet show."

Although Tieck criticizes some of the ideas of his day, he is still writing within its conventions. For example, with two hunchback characters, he depicts how physical deformity was treated as an outward sign of inward evil. One is described as an "imp of hell"; for the other, an accused witch, the hunchback "made her ugliness still more disgusting. Poor wretch, doomed from birth to be accused of foul deeds for no more than an unfortunate demeanor." The sense of injustice here sounds like an attack on prejudice, but it still deems her "disgusting" for it, and the narrative bears out that the prejudice does in fact reflect their inwardly sinful natures.

The two stories by Erckmann-Chatrian have a different tone. Written later in the century and set in recognizable urban environments, they begin to have a hint of *Weird Tales* about them. "The Eye Invisible," in which an artist sees evidence of crime or witchcraft from his garret window, is reminiscent of Robert W. Chambers's *King in Yellow* stories, and "The Child Stealer," a gruesome crime thriller, also feels a bit more modern. In his introduction, Rutherford likens it to *The Texas Chainsaw Massacre,* which turns out to be pretty apt.

The survival of Gothic literature into the present day is a reminder that the afterlife of a work can be longer than we realize. While so much has changed, so much else hasn't. Older works can have continued relevance, as these tales of isolated villages and bygone social codes express aspects of human nature that are still with us today. Some of these are understandable impulses: the tendency to view real individuals through a distorting lens of idealism, to dream of an ideal world, to seek personal pleasure rather than more meaningful occupations. These drives aren't intrinsically wrong, but can, as in so many of these stories, lead to dark consequences.

A Literary Journal on the Fringe

Tony Fonseca

S. T. JOSHI, ed. *Penumbra* No. 2 (2021). New York: Hippo-campus Press. 310 pp. $20.00 tpb. ISBN 9781614983095. $6.00 ebook, ISBN 9781614983149.

A penumbra is a space of partial illumination, one that exists between the perfect shadow on all sides and the full light. Or to put it another way, it is a surrounding or adjoining region in which something exists in a lesser degree. In other words, it is the fringe. It is therefore the apt title of a literary journal that deals with horror and dark fantasy. Published once a year, in summer, *Penumbra* publishes short stories, poetry, and scholarly articles. It is edited by esteemed horror scholar S. T. Joshi, so the quality of much of the work included is of the highest standard.

Penumbra put out its second issue, the focus of this review, this past summer, and it is a remarkable 310-page collection of renowned short story authors and poets such as Ramsey Campbell, Darrell Schweitzer, and Leigh Blackmore, legends such as Algernon Blackwood and Guy de Maupassant, and well-known scholars such as John C. Tibbetts and Joshi himself. In fact, *Penumbra* stands out from the horror literature crowd because of its scholarly articles, with this issue addressing the influences and thematic concerns of such luminaries as Caitlín R. Kiernan, Greg Bear, Guy de Maupassant, Lord Dunsany, Clark Ashton Smith, William Hope Hodgson, Algernon Blackwood, and of course, H. P. Lovecraft.

Among the short stories, Campbell's "Lost for Words," Mark Samuels's "The Interminable Abomination," and Schweitzer's "All Kings and Princes Bow Down unto Me" are the issue's standout pieces. In addition, the issue offers a reprint of an early Algernon Blackwood ghost story (likely his first ever published story), "A Mysterious House," originally published in *Belgravia* (July 1889).

Campbell's "Lost for Words" tells the story of horror author (he is actually more of a dark humorist) Roy Stafford, famous for his Barney the Vampire creation. Stafford meets a mysterious fellow author named Charles Vane while signing his story at an author's table, and Vane is very specific about what he wants a featured author to inscribe: "From one writing soul to another." Stafford obliges and shakes Vane's hand, which he describes as spongy, a surface that seems permeable and absorbent. He soon realizes that he has given up his soul, as he loses his ability to formulate words and sentences. As is typical of Campbell, the tale is masterfully written and fiendishly clever as well as metatextual, as it turns out that Vane has been turned down by Stafford's editor, Asha, who did not want to publish his book about a vampire who feeds on language without rewrites that Vane was not willing to make. By the end of the story, Stafford can barely articulate one sentence, a fate that no writer would ever wish for.

"The Interminable Abomination" is a brilliant story about a cursed book. Samuels's narrator, a seasoned bookseller who has enjoyed a thirty-year career in the trade of selling bought books at a small profit, notes that he has never been inspired to write anything himself, a fact that will ultimately lead to the tale's final irony. He receives a query from a former customer, Colonel Archibald Dowson, a former colonel in the British Army who was stationed in Burma during the Second World War and is notorious for his obsession with horrors—the more nightmarish, the better. It is also rumored that he "perfected acts of hideously refined cruelty against captured soldiers of the Imperial Japanese Army." Upon arriving at Dowson's, the narrator discovers that the colonel is a somewhat ghoulish-looking ancient man, and that he has already sold most of his valuable books to the narrator's rival. However, he does still have a rare book titled *Unknown Nightmares,* which contains an anonymous story titled "The Interminable Abomination," which the narrator begins to read. He then begins suffering from nightmares. As it turns out, the colonel has marked him for the anonymous story's next victim, his Asian wife being the last one. As the colonel tells him, "It's never the same story when read twice: it changes constantly and takes more and more of the life from its readers." The narrator is now fated to live the rest of his life typing up his nightmares for the colonel's pleasure, as his brain slowly rots.

Schweitzer's "All Kings and Princes Bow Down unto Me" is a masterful fairytale-inspired horror story about a teenage girl named Anna who, thanks to a chance encounter with The Grim Reaper on a night well before she is fated to die, is forced to become his apprentice. Anna grows into the apprenticeship well and even concocts a simple plan to distract Death so that she might kill him and take his place, becoming "awesomely beautiful, but dreaded by all." In the wonderful scene after she does exactly that, Death becomes a sympathetic character: "For a brief instant a voice seemed to whisper, 'At last. I was so tired. Now I am free,' but then there wasn't even dust, or bones, just a few bits of the cloak, which blew away like the ashes of burnt leaves."

Other stories in the issue include Geoffrey Reiter's "A Green Shade," Manuel Arenas's "The Dream of a Dead Poet," Shawn Phelps's "Quiet," Katherine Kerestman's "Markovia," Maxwell I. Gold's "Summa Oblivia," Curtis M. Lawson's "A Grave at the End of the World," Scott J. Couturier's "Like Vultures," and Scott Bradfield's "The Holiday Transmission." While Reiter creates memorable imagery in his tale about a modern-day witch (who survived the Puritan era) who controls a forest and is capable of turning animals, including human beings, into trees and other foliage, he seems to pull his punches when he has the two main characters, Isabella and Abigail, manage to escape the seemingly inescapable. Arenas's, Gold's, and Couturier's tales are simply dream visions. Although all three have some memorable imagery, they left me wanting some kind of narrative, something more than a collection of images. Phelps's "Quiet," the tale of a young girl who is destined to become a religious sacrifice, has a lot of potential but lacks the development necessary to make it a stand-out story. Kerestman's "Markovia" has promise but reads more like sword-and-sorcery fantasy than Count Dracula–based vampire horror. It does contain some crisp imagery; however, the story does not quite fascinate, perhaps due to its predictability or perhaps due to a lack of sympathetic characterization (so in the end, I was not moved or horrified). Lawson's "A Grave at the End of the World," a science fiction story about a secret experiment to create the perfect assassin, ostensibly to prevent Armageddon, suffers because the real purpose of the experiments is never clear. I had only a vague idea why any of the action occurs. It doesn't help that the story's protagonist/hero, Providence, and its surprising bad-guy-turned-good-guy, Dr. Wallach, are both underdeveloped characters. And Bradfield's "The Holiday Transmission," the tale of a socialist-leaning man, Arnold Simonson, who is haunted by his dead father, a former CEO and controlling stockholder capitalist who was known for his disdain for anyone who did not value money above all else, does have interesting hauntings through telecommunications devices; however, the reason for the haunting is never made clear, and the story suffers for it. The implication is that the haunting is done simply to ridicule and annoy Simonson, but if that is the case, the story loses its chance to be either disquieting or powerful.

Among the standout scholarly articles, *Penumbra* offers James Goho's "Spooky Action across Time: Caitlín R. Kiernan's Fiction Disturbs Noël Carroll's Philosophy of Horror," Tibbetts's "'Music in the Blood': Greg Bear and the Gothic Imagination," Kyla Lee Ward's "Vampire Poetry," Joshi's "Guy de Maupassant: Women, Madness, and the Horla," and Lee Weinstein's "Hodgson, *The Night Land*, and William Morris."

In his study of Kiernan's fiction, Goho cites stories such as "As Red as Red" (2010), "The Wolf Who Cried Girl" (2007), "For One Who Has Lost Herself" (2006), and "To This Water (Johnstown, Pennsylvania 1889)" (1996), among others, arguing that the stories' monsters challenge Carroll's theory in *The Philosophy of Horror; or, Paradoxes of the Heart* (1990) that in order for a monster to exist, it must be threatening, repulsive, and unsympathetic, as well as "unclean and disgusting." Goho gives various examples, such as from "As Red as Red," wherein Abby Gladding, the imaginary vampire, is a sympathetic character who helps Ms. Howard "to navigate her transitions between fantasy and reality and between estrangement and acceptance." Goho notes of "The Wolf Who Cried Girl" that the story's wolf/girl evokes sympathy, not revulsion, which falls instead on the human character.

Tibbetts's contribution reads much like an homage to Bear, but it is so chock full of wonderful observations and memories that it is an absolute pleasure to read. His main argument is that despite Bear's flirtations with science fiction (he calls this Bear's fearlessly treading "the spaceways in his galaxy devouring epics of science, hardware, and apocalyptic events"), the core tropes of the Gothic narrative never wavers in his works. He gives the examples of Faustian pacts, hungry ghosts, quests for forbidden knowledge, and the transformative powers of music. As an example, he discusses *Vitals* (2002), a novel about the quest for eternal life, a cautionary tale where the "results are the horrific transformation of not just his body but that of others and, ultimately, the world itself."

Ward's "Vampire Poetry" is an excellent study of the evolution of vampire poetry, mainly in England and the United States, although other countries are studied as well. Using the example of Yeats, she notes the various conventions of vampire fiction that lend themselves to poetry: "a combination of sex and death, the conflicting emotions of fear and desire, [and] the trappings of darkness, antiquity, and superstition." She begins her study with the oldest known poem that mentions a vampire, "Der Vampire," by Heinrich August Ossenfelder; then examines poems by Johann Ludwig Tieck, E. T. A. Hoffmann, Lord Byron, Henry Thomas Liddle, Robert Southey, Théophile Gautier, James Clerk Maxwell, and a myriad of others, ending on the more modern vampire poetry authors, Frederick Seidel, Denise Dumar, Michael R. Collings, Marge Simon, and Dawn R. Cotter, as well as Singaporean poet Christina Sng.

S. T. Joshi's "Guy de Maupassant: Women, Madness, and the Horla" examines the weird works of de Maupassant, which Joshi notes does constitute a relatively small proportion of his total output. However, as Joshi points out, these works are interesting because they highlight "the complex intertwining of his life, psychological makeup, and literary theory in ways that his more mainstream writing does not." Joshi then gives biographical details of de Maupassant's life, from his being encouraged to write short stories by Flaubert to his earliest known work that makes use of the weird ("Le Docteur Héraclius Gloss"), to his writings on Poe, to his first foray into horror, the poem "Terreur" (1880, with de Maupassant's first genuine weird tale, "Sur l'eau," following in 1881). Joshi traces the development of the weird in de Maupassant's work, concluding with "Le Horla" (1887), de Maupassant's greatest contribution to weird fiction. Joshi also provides a bibliography of Guy de Maupassant's weird tales. In a separate entry, Joshi also provides a translation of de Maupassant's "The Fantastic," which was first published in *Le Gaulois* in October 1883.

Weinstein's "Hodgson, *The Night Land*, and William Morris" looks at the novel "often considered to be William Hope Hodgson's magnum opus," *The Night Land* (1912). Weinstein argues that it defies simple categorization: it can be considered science fiction, supernatural horror, and heroic fantasy. It is the last of these categories that is the impetus of the article, as Weinstein argues that the novel is at heart a heroic quest, bearing more than a passing resemblance to a medieval romance. His thesis is that Hodgson was greatly influenced by William Morris's novel *The Well at the World's End* (1896), a heroic fantasy set in an imaginary medieval world. Presenting evidence of the similarities in the two novels, he concludes that Hodgson took the trope of the medieval quest and transplanted it to a future age.

Other articles include Mairead Drake's "The Almost-Nonhuman: Life and Death in Kelly Link, Carmen Maria Machado, and George Saunders," David Rose's "Free Will vs. Love: John Collier and Brian McNaughton," Martin Wangsgaard Jürgensen's "A Matter of Belief: Further Thoughts on Lord Dunsany and Religion," Cecelia Hopkins-Drewer's "'The Quest of Iranon' and *Don Rodriguez*: Two Exercises in the Picaresque," and Ian Fetters's "Icy Portents of Doom: Clark Ashton Smith's Hyperborean Cycle and the Polar Myth." Drake's article argues that many slipstream texts contain characters, namely ghosts, zombies, and humanoid entities, who blur the distinction between what is human and what is not; furthermore he notes that these characters are often used to explore the concept of humanity by breaking it.

Rose's article elaborates on two comments by S. T. Joshi dealing with McNaughton's unique voice and his being better than his chief influence, Clark Aston Smith, as well as a remark by McNaughton himself about his lack of confidence in his writing. Rose concludes that "McNaughton is as good and, in certain ways, surpasses many of his beloved predecessors," especially Smith, as McNaughton could examine "deep conundrums with masterful narrative skill." Jürgensen argues that a number of themes in Lord Dunsany's writing still need further exploration, namely that of his stance on religion as well as his own possible religiosity. He notes that "it is surprising because gods and religion were from the very outset part of Dunsany's fictional world, and the theme has accordingly to some extent been touched upon by nearly all his commentators." He further argues that there has been a good deal of "analytical imprecision" on the role of religion. His article then proceeds to enumerate instances of religion in them. Hopkins-Drewer investigates the picaresque mode as used in "The Quest of Iranon" by H. P. Lovecraft and *Don Rodriguez: Chronicles of Shadow Valley* by Lord Dunsany. She argues that "while Dunsany's and Lovecraft's stories both appear to have elements of the picaresque, in the final examination the discussion will conclude each author has created his own permutations." Fetters's article examines Clark Ashton Smith's Hyperborean Cycle tales, beginning with "'The Tale of Satampra Zeiros'" (1929), and goes on to look at the twelve other Smith tales concerned with Hyperborea, described as "a kind of proto-Arctic, mythic space that was said to have flourished during the Miocene era approximately fifteen million years in the past."

Among the standout poetry in this issue, readers will find Adam Bolivar's "When Old Gods Rattle Chains," Ann K. Schwader's "Waiting in Carcosa," Geoffrey Reiter's "The Absence," and Leigh Blackmore's "Basilisk Eye." Schwader's "Waiting in Carcosa" is of particular interest as it is a rare horror-themed villanelle. Reiter's is one of the issue's best poems, containing lines such as

She haunts me in her absences. The breath
I once felt warm upon my nape is frozen
Without her bright noonlight white smile, the loosing
Of grinning pale teeth through her lips (a wreath
Of mistletoe). . . .

Despite some of the problems noted in this review, I thoroughly enjoyed this issue of *Penumbra*. I believe it will be a boon to horror fans and scholars of the weird tale. Moreover, it will add significantly to S. T. Joshi's legacy as one of the preeminent scholars of weird fiction, as well as one of its best advocates.

Ramsey's Rant: Living Liverpool

Ramsey Campbell

Liverpool brought me to life as a writer. I was born there in 1946 and moved across the river to Wallasey in 1981, a relocation local purists see as abandoning Scouseness. I think I've retained however much of that I had in the first place. I'm still on Merseyside, literally so, with a view of that river from my desk. The area has been at the core of my stories for most of my career.

August Derleth began that, not just by publishing my tales but by initially advising me to transfer them from Lovecraft's Massachusetts to Britain. When he suggested the Severn Valley I made haste to obey. Decades later it occurred to me that I needn't have taken his advice so literally—Chester and its environs were just an hour away by rail, and quite as steeped in Roman history as Gloucestershire. Since I'd never visited that area, the depiction of it in my early tales isn't much more accurate than my version of New England was, but I assume Derleth didn't notice. That first collection largely keeps reality at bay, but as soon as I'd completed it my fiction edged closer to lived experience. Despite lingering in Brichester, both "The Stone on the Island" and "The Childish Fear" drew upon the tax office where I worked (London Provincial 1 at 72 Church Street in Liverpool). Reading Nabokov as I turned seventeen liberated my language in "The Stone on the Island", but I soon lost my sense of this and spent most of two years in producing awkward first drafts (later rewritten from scratch). It was only when my bookseller friend John Roles introduced me to the location of "The Cellars" in 1965 that I regained my creative grasp.

The cellars under Rumford Place (an area now changed almost beyond recognition) weren't just the setting for the story; they were its inspiration. Except for the uncanny elements, they were exactly as described in the tale. They inspired me to depict the route through downtown Liverpool to them as well, and all the details there are real, although largely historical by now. It may have been the drive towards authenticity that encouraged me to portray a colleague and draw on my short-lived relationship with her. The sense of place, which is to say the sense of Liverpool, is crucial to the story. It's the first one I take to be wholly my own.

Instinctive writing has its strengths but drawbacks too. Soon my awareness of what I'd done in "The Cellars" deserted me, and I reverted to producing unwieldy first drafts. In the case of the initial draft of "Concussion", even the Merseyside locations didn't let me engage fully with the material. What instinct led me to revisit Brichester for the final version of "Cold Print"? The city in the tale is Liverpool in all but name. The ploy appears to have consolidated my sense of Merseyside along with a commitment to observation, so that the final draft of "Concussion" stays much closer to the holiday dalliance on which it was based, locations and all.

Several years passed before I returned home in my tales, and perhaps that's one reason why some of the stories that followed *Demons by Daylight* seem to be floundering in search of a technique if not a theme. In 1969 "The Christmas Present", written at speed as a seasonal ghost story for the local BBC, gains some inspiration from the graveyard of the Anglican cathedral, but it's a flimsy item. "The Whining" also inhabits Liverpool 8 but conveys little of its flavour, while "The Height of the Scream" touches on the kind of artist Liverpool was celebrating at the time, although the painter in the tale hasn't much in common with my old friend Adrian Henri (who once reviewed *Demons by Daylight* for the local journal *Arts Alive,* confessing bewilderment with "Concussion"). Perhaps I needed the spur of a dedicated career to make me connect with my environment. Certainly when I went fulltime in mid-1973, our immediate district saved the day, and "The Man in the Underpass" arose from the graffiti in the pedestrian subway closest to our house.

Once again I seem to have missed the implications of the inspiration. Several stories transpired before I had recourse to another Merseyside site, and then only because I was casting about somewhat desperately for material. The result—set in

New Brighton without naming the area, because the route between the real fairgrounds didn't fit my needs—was "The Companion". After several feeble fitful bids at science fiction and a somewhat more successful venture into fantasy I infested a house very much like ours at 54 Buckingham Road in Tuebrook with projections of a neighbour's psychedelic experiences (in fact my own if anyone's, but I assume the neighbours never noticed) in "Through the Walls". "Baby" took me back to the Granby Street district behind our first apartment (at 25 Princes Avenue), and much more was to be had of it. The area became the core of *The Doll Who Ate His Mother*.

My early teens were strewn with uncompleted novels—three, at any rate—and the prospect of completing one let it sprawl, even though it was plotted in advance. I walked through locations I planned to use. It's my experience that if you visit your settings you can always find details that will be relevant to your tale, but you have to look for yourself. Just the same, Clare's walk through Newsham Park signifies little more than my release from the strictures of shorter fiction. By contrast, the derelict territory she braves in the climactic chapters is exactly what I viewed in 1975, and in *Danse Macabre* Stephen King enthused about the depiction of the district and of the wider city: ". . . perhaps the central character here is Liverpool itself . . . the picture he draws of it gives the reader the feeling that he is observing a slumbering, semisentient monster that *might* awake at any moment."

"The Invocation" returns to the Princes Avenue apartments, and "The Brood" includes the views from our windows there. Did I really see a woman circling around a streetlamp? I no longer recall. Apparently loath to abandon the apartment, I rented it to Cathy and Peter for the duration of *The Face That Must Die,* but the local inspirations of the novel lie elsewhere. I'd learned that a friend who lived in Cantril Farm, the overspill estate near Liverpool, had come home one night only to be unable to locate his house in the maze of anonymous streets. When I toured the area I found it as bewildering as John Horridge would. My portrait of the area from which he'd been rehoused was closely observed too, though I was already familiar with that progressively derelict district from searching for suburban cinemas in my teens. Indeed, the area was one essence of my personal Liverpool.

"Mackintosh Willy" returns us to Tuebrook, where Newsham Park is diagonally opposite the haunted underpass. By now, like my Liverpool 8, the area was growing as variously uncanny as Arkham. The tale grew out of two sights in the park: footprints in the concrete that surrounded a pool and graffiti in a shelter. My narrator has the experience I had—misperceiving the graffiti as a solitary man's name—which was enough to lodge in one of the notebooks I'd learned to carry. Chrissie Maher and her community newspaper were real too. Indeed, in the early seventies she asked me to review films for it, and I can't remember why this came to nothing. Later she founded the Plain English Campaign, for which John Moores University awarded her an honorary fellowship.

The Parasite ranges wider around Liverpool, but I believe it was this book that prompted Charles L. Grant to comment that I was using the area too much (just as, according to Charlie, he tended to default too readily to Oxrun Station). Years later an editor (not one I worked with) informed me that fiction set in northern England was unlikely to sell well. The merits of rooting your tales in your lived environment outweigh all that, I believe, but Charlie's observation persuaded me to set *The Nameless* and *The Claw* elsewhere. As for *The Parasite,* the scene at the Aigburth tip is founded on a walk I took there after dark. If I'd delayed a few years I might have encountered Clive Barker's Mama Pus.

Although "The Show Goes On" doesn't name Liverpool, I had the Hippodrome cinema in mind. Built as a music hall, it preserved a labyrinth of corridors and dressing-rooms behind the screen, a territory into which I strayed one night, having taken a wrong turn on the way to an exit. Deep in the maze I came up against a pair of fire doors, and as I made to unlock the bar that held them I saw through the slit between them several figures rising from the floor in the lurid dimness to meet me. I retreated at speed and didn't look back. By the time the cinema closed, the local BBC had hired me as a film reviewer, which earned me an invitation to a farewell party. Although we guests were given a free run of the place, I couldn't find the doors I'd flinched from opening.

"The Ferries" was my bid to convey the strangeness of Parkgate, a fishing village that now looks out on a river of grass. Who knows why the image of a boat took many years to suggest itself? Perhaps my subconscious, which I'd frequently searched for suggestions, needed to be left alone to do its job. In the thirties G. G. Pendarves, another *Weird Tales* writer living on the Wirral, set "Thing of Darkness" in the village, which she renamed Seagate. Our two tales demonstrate how almost half a century changed the landscape.

"The Depths" uses Liverpool for convenience, bearing out Charlie Grant's objection, you may think. "This Time" took me to Birkenhead Park, an inspiration for New York's Central Park, at night to walk a route the protagonist would follow. "Calling Card" is resolutely local, having been commissioned by the Liverpool *Daily Post* for the paper's Christmas special. The story was to span the period from Christmas Eve to New Year's and to employ all the Merseyside locations it could. Several gave me ideas, some of which proved too gruesome for the editor. Subsequently his replacement approached me for a Christmas ghost story, and perhaps tastes had changed, since the tale was published without demur.

Incarnate brings some chapters home, and I believe I was celebrating its completion when the landlord of the Baltic Fleet on Liverpool's dock road asked me to write a tale for his pub magazine. The result was "Watch the Birdie". The succeeding years saw local locations crop up in *The Influence* and *The Count of Eleven*, but I believe Merseyside was more crucial to *The Last Voice They Hear*. That novel was conceived under duress, out of apparent necessity when my agents warned me horror had died in the marketplace. My British agent advised setting out to write like Thomas Harris, but I can only write like myself, which requires engaging my imagination. Founding scenes in locales I revisited helped it to focus, and soon enough the book resembled one I might have written as a natural development.

Secret Story let me have some fun with local stuff. For *Thieving Fear* I found my favourite walk on Merseyside ideal. That's the sandstone ridge and heath and woods at Thurstaston, although it wasn't until Virgin reprinted the novel that an editor spotted I'd misnamed the place Thursaston—I'd been misreading the signposts for decades. Charlotte's climactic nocturnal journey up the Wirral Way was mine. I'd previously used that countryside walk at the start of "Again", which makes me aware how I've changed. Once I was the longhaired intruder viewed askance by regulars, but now I'm an elderly regular who acts—I hope not too possessively—like one.

While "Peep" might be less without its Merseyside locations, *Creatures of the Pool* wouldn't exist at all. In some ways it's my ultimate Liverpool novel. I researched it for decades, buying books about the town—the more obscure the better—whenever I found them. Several of the nineteenth-century tomes I drew upon appear never to have been reprinted. Over the years I filled notebooks with material deriving from the books. Some information I simply transcribed, but other notes developed ideas I found. In quite a few cases I can no longer distinguish tales or traditions I invented from those I read about and used. I would be delighted if parts of the novel become the kind of legend it seeks to evoke.

The territory of "Chucky Comes to Liverpool" is psychological, although the mind and its surroundings can seldom be disentangled in my tales. It deals with an unexpected side effect of the murder of James Bulger, a tragic case in which a toddler was tortured and murdered by two ten-year-olds. Despite no mention of films in the evidence, the judge blamed violent videos, and the *Sun* newspaper tried to ingratiate itself with Scousers (having permanently antagonised them by printing lies about the Hillsborough football tragedy) by campaigning against a *Child's Play* film. All this lent the video the status of a malevolent legend, and my story was a bid to counteract this with a sense of the truth.

The Seven Days of Cain shows my subconscious at work. Once I had the concept of the book in mind I settled on a location (Crosby) to which I could drive whenever I needed to remind myself of details or discover new ones. It hadn't occurred to me—to my conscious mind, at any rate—how thematically relevant the sculptures on the nearby beach were, though I was aware of them. I've come to believe that if my imagination is engaged with the characters and the situation, the symbolic structure of the narrative tends to take care of itself, organised by my subconscious.

"The Rounds", a snapshot of contemporary paranoia, suggested itself on the Merseyside underground railway, and so that's where it takes place, though the threat is global. *The Kind Folk* demonstrates the worth of visiting your settings whenever you can; there turned out to be a spiritualist church within sight of the street where I'd chosen to house a character. *The Pretence* takes place in a Liverpool altered in ways the reader must decide—perhaps not much.

"On the Tour" could scarcely be more Scouse, and the domestic location hardly matters. *Think Yourself Lucky* ranges around Merseyside in its feral quest, but how exaggerated are its targets? Although I call three recent books my Brichester Mythos trilogy, the novels that comprise the trio are profoundly Liverpudlian, *The Searching Dead* in particular. It reaches deep into the Liverpool of my early adolescence and evokes the times and the experiences as precisely as it can. Together with *Creatures of the Pool*, I'd say it was my ultimate tribute to my hometown.

It hasn't exhausted the possibilities. *The Wise Friend* perches its protagonist above New Brighton Station, which adds an eloquent motif. *Somebody's Voice* would be less vivid without its Wallasey specifics. The most recent case of local inspiration, "Wherever You Look", makes me realise that all these three depend on the Wirral peninsula. It has many legends. Perhaps it's time I pondered a novel, a *Creatures of the Pool* for this side of the river. You heard about it here first, if it comes to fruition.

How the Wind Twists Between Stars

Leigh Blackmore

ANN K. SCHWADER. *Unquiet Stars*. Central Point, OR: Weird House, 2021. 82 pp. $14.95 tpb. ISBN 9781888993073.

Whether in free verse or metrical formalism, Ann K. Schwader has long been the dark mistress of modern weird verse, well deserving her status as an SFPA Grand Master (2018).

In this new collection, her ninth, the centerpiece is a nine-sonnet interpretation of H. G. Wells's classic novel of weird animality and scientific experimentation, *The Island of Dr Moreau*. Schwader's sequence is titled *Faces from the House of Pain*. Perhaps it was my own attraction to the themes of Wells's novel (which led me in the late 1990s to have the tattoo on my left shoulder inked at a parlor in Annandale, Sydney, called "The House of Pain") that drew me to read this sequence first, of all the poems in this volume. One mark of Schwader's poetic mastery is her eschewing of the obvious in this sequence. Rather than simply retelling the events of the novel, she remakes the story through her verse, as Moreau remade his creatures, amplifying its philosophical underpinnings about what it means to be beast and what it means to be human.

Like the *Faces from the House of Pain* sequence, a number of poems appear in this collection for the first time. "Midnight in the Hot Zone" is a short, sharp shock of a verse with the theme "Our tribe is virus." "Past Equinox" uses similar patterns of repeating phrase and image to depict shifting balance, failing light and ascendant night. "Pink Crosses" is subtitled "Ciudad Juarez" (the name of the most populous city in Chihuahua, Mexico). One of the most dangerous cities in the world, largely due to brutal violence between rival drug cartels, Ciudad Juarez has seen hundreds of women murdered. Schwader's poem is an oblique but powerful tribute to these lost lives, which are commemorated by pink crosses planted outside the student union at the University of Utah. "Sepulcher of Saints" seems a clear declaration of conventional religious faith, deeply felt. "Snatching Shadows" is another meditation on death, this time from the angle of poets and poetry, particularly that of John Keats, but is not easy of interpretation. "Star-Tide," the first poem in the volume, hints at apocalypse, and at Klarkashtonian dooms beyond time. Situated somewhere between prose poem and free verse, "Stone Tongue" seems to address the impossibility of language to capture the actual, the stillness of voice that accompanies observation of the natural world which itself speaks louder than any human word. Schwader's love of archaeology is present here, along with shades of Samuel Beckett. "Unquiet Stars," which closes the volume, highlights Schwader's equal devotion to science-fictional imagination as to weirdness; it is predicated on scientific explorations but slyly suggestive of alien horrors that may await beyond the "unquiet stars." Victrola (At the End of the World)" is almost post-apocalyptic—"there is no power now"—and draws on Schwader's frequent motif of a threatening encroachment of darkness, and humanity's insignificance: "Thin and cold as coyotes within our concrete myth"; yet there may be a qualified optimism in its concluding lines.

Unquiet Stars is rich with other verses, collected from a wide variety of magazines and anthologies ranging from *Abyss & Apex* to *Weird Fiction Review*. Some are utterly original mixtures of the scientific and the ghostly ("Corridors Enough") and others homages to familiar fictional mythologies—Robert W. Chambers ("All Masks Are Mirrors," "Deep Winter Skies"), H. P. Lovecraft ("A Wizard's Daughter," "Haunted Innsmouth"), and ancient Egypt ("Last Justice," "The Thirst of Sekhmet," "Tomb-Feasters"). Witchcraft, ancient cultures of South America (Aztec, Nahuatl, Belize), the SETI program of space exploration, entropy, far horizons, deep hauntings, endless oceans, the sands of Mars—all are grist to Schwader's poetic mill, in a dazzling variety of poetic forms.

Weird House, a relatively new publisher and one to watch, has done immeasurable service to devotees of horror and speculative poetry by putting into print Ann K. Schwader's latest collection, which surely belongs on every self-respecting horror enthusiast's shelf.

Breach

Dan Raskin

I.

It first beset the radiation berms at the periphery of the city, which one day appeared to have been colonized by unworldly organic structures spanning the full width of an embankment. Absorbance function did not seem to be affected, but all radioactive waste transfer was ceased as a precaution. Irradiation spikes plagued the city for several days until the structures disappeared, along with half of each affected berm's absorbance capacity.

The second occurrence was documented in an agricultural region far away from the city. An irrigation well was replaced by columns of delicate white filaments that resembled the lateral sprawl of archaic center-pivots. The filaments, shimmering in the breeze, could not be cut. For weeks, columns of similar size and properties appeared in fields proximate to the first, until fading back out of existence along with the originary wells. In a nearby district, thick mats of the same filaments were found ringing the oil palms in three non-contiguous plantations. They too were impervious to intervention and slowly disintegrated into the soil, leaving no trace other than decaying grass where the mat had lain.

Soon, more disruptive instances were documented. Hollow, adhesive spheres burst from sewage drains in the city's waste processing district, as if the streets themselves were spewing a long-hibernating brood. The spheres accumulated until they began collapsing under their own weight and seeped back into the sewers, clogging them briefly before vanishing. At a solar plant, sheets of translucent fibers floated above the panels, oozing a caustic fluid. It was discovered that the sheets could be burned. This, however, resulted in the same sheets growing back, albeit thicker than before and producing more of the caustic ooze-fluid. Eventually, after expanding along the power lines for several kilometers, the sheets thinned and vaporized.

Most instances passed in and out of observable existence without generating mass panic. The firms chartered to manage the city's fixed infrastructure contained spillover damage with sufficient efficacy, and the Council was able to restrict the flow of information to the general public. Still, friction from below was increasing, and the Council bodies and firm executives agreed they had to respond decisively. A theory had to be developed, and action had to be taken.

By whatever methods of evaluation and discourse, it was decided that what was plaguing their society and threatening their regime was neither a protracted event nor an anomalous cosmological phenomenon, but a *thing*. A discrete *it,* breaching into existence. It must have origin, patterns, structure, and most importantly, limits. Therefore, it could be modeled, understood, and if not destroyed, then at least controlled. The Council asserted its leadership in this pursuit, owing to its long-standing monopolization of computational processing power. An investigation program was commissioned, and teams of investigators were sent to document, record, and collect data on Its manifestations as they occurred.

Almost immediately after the commission began work, the frequency of the breaches began to synchronize, and the spatial distribution narrowed. Regular, detailed study became simpler to coordinate. Investigators soon observed clustered breaches converging into a single zone of continuous anomalous activity, spanning a region of low foothills previously used for wind generation. The shifting of forms did not stop. The zone would be haunted by forests of dust spires, dunes made of rainbow-hued plastic fibers, or knotted stacks of sinew and wood for days or weeks at a time, until a new form would manifest.

The spatial stability of the breaches quickly perceived to be a preferred state of affairs, as there would be fewer infrastructural catastrophes. If it stayed in one spot, at least it could be studied and perhaps even contained. This latter concept gained adherents in the Council chambers with close relationships with the technological security firms, who petitioned the Council for funds to construct a containment barrier. The theories bolstering this course of action were highly contested, but the deluge of proposals, plans, and urgent appeals to existential crises overwhelmed the concerned chatter of the network administrators. A hybrid of two proposals was prepared, and a containment system was devised based on a mesh network of partial-spectrum reflectors and signal dampening buffers. To appease the network's concerns that containment was an expensive, rash, and potentially counterproductive approach, the firms also agreed to fund round-the-clock general data collection and variance monitoring.

Teams were hired to scout the perimeter and interior of the zone, but severe restrictions were placed on technical methods of recording and transmitting data. Initial excitement and optimism about the prospect of understanding and the breach gave way to stagnation as the regularity of form mutations adhered to no legible pattern; the anomalous and otherwise impossible physical phenomena documented using one methodology could not be verified using another. Despite the completion of the containment system, the breach perimeter began to expand.

But as often happens when the veneer of certainty fractures the surface of official dogma, new theories emerged among those whose proximity to the breach differed from those whose fears and conceptions first structured the response to the crisis.

II.

"Fast. That's what it looks like when you visualize it."

"Hanid, that's not what I asked."

"Yeah, but it's still the first thing about it. It's fast. And big."

"Of course it's big. We're in a breach. It's huge. But fast? What does that even . . . I just want to know how come we have come out every day and do all this . . ." Brin threw his hands up, gesturing to the forest of tangled, fluorescent tubes that covered the hillside.

". . . witnessing?"

"Whatever you want to call it. Take records on this shit that we can't even . . . It keeps changing! The readings are nonsense!"

"Well that's kind of the point, right? We're in a *breach*. It *changes*. And we *witness* it."

"No, I mean, yeah . . . of course. I meant what they say we have to do; they keep saying it's for different reasons. And anyway, it's not like the breach is *actually* being contained."

"Right. They're just afraid of getting it right, I think. But it's pretty clear to me that what we're doing is witnessing, whether they know it or not. That's it."

"Remember when they told us to go in and count *all* the new structures. . . . At that point it had changed to these shaking log things that were soaking wet, even though it hadn't rained. The ground was mud and we kept slipping. What a nightmare."

"Ha, you're still sore about that one. I was on that other assignment, remember? But what I mean, if we're counting, recording, describing, documenting—"

"—mapping . . ."

"Mapping, whatever. I don't care what they think they're getting out of this. We're still just witnessing, and *that*'s what's important."

"What's important to me is that we don't waste *all* morning arguing about objectives. I was only whining. I didn't mean to get you going on this. But I'm serious about banking these work credits. I know you're not, but still. I want to be able to take some time *off,* maybe even save up to move out of the district if things start getting . . ." Brin paused, unsure if he wanted to speculate, even in abstract terms, on a possible trajectory. "We're starting mapping today, so let's do the perimeter." He handed Hanid the tablet and stylus. "You mark, I'll dictate."

Hanid took the tablet and started walking along the perimeter. "Sure, got it. But you *did* ask, Brin. so I'm telling you—"

"What you *think?*"

"—what I'm telling you! What I've seen! So just listen. We're out here doing all *this*"—she waved her arms wildly—"because it needs a witness. Otherwise it won't stay put, like it didn't before. And the Council . . . the Council thinks they need to *do* something. They don't want to admit that they have no clue what it is or how to even see it. So they keep sending us out here." Hanid rolled her eyes.

"It's spreading though. Isn't that—"

"Better it spreads than it doesn't stay put. That's what the Council says. It's stayed in one place since the containment, so they think it's *working*. But that's not what's even keeping it, and it's spreading. The *breach* is *breaching*. My point is that *it*—the *thing* that's breaching—needs witnessing, and what I'm trying to tell you is that we can *actually do that*. We've actually *been* doing that."

"Hold it, I've got some readouts for you. Record: Six meters west of the four-thirteen limit, two Manifests. Pipe-looking things . . ." Brin held the differential multi-meter within a few centimeters of the nearest tube, and carefully noted the output. " . . . and it's cold. Wow, it's really cold, like, twenty below freezing." He scanned the second one. "And this one is slightly warmer than air temperature. Twenty eight. Got all that?"

"Sure. We're just mapping today though. I thought you were trying to *get this done* and not waste time doing another week's work." Hanid smiled.

"This is *part* of mapping. Perimeter differentials. You *know* that. Maybe another crew is sampling from the interior today, I don't know."

"They are. Kama and Adam." Hanid grinned even wider. "Anyways . . . and listen this time if you want any of this to make sense. It doesn't care if we know anything about it, and we shouldn't care either because there's nothing we can do except show up and see it as it is. And, yeah, it changes all the time blah blah, but that's because most of us aren't interested in seeing what it's actually like. But I'm telling you, that's why we're here. And as long as we are, we can try and see it. I have and what I'm saying is it's *fast*."

"Fine, heard. Now why don't we make like *it* and *get moving*. I want to get this done on time today. No overtime. So let's go, huh? *FAST!*" Brin shot an annoyed look back at Hanid, who, laughing, quickened her stride to match his. There was another set of tube-things thirty paces out, and a lot more ahead of those.

*

"Four count, two branching, spectrum A.67, temp differentials six point three, ten point oh, thirty one point seven, fifteen point two—"

"Got it. Hey, it's past sixth watch. Wanna eat?" Hanid dropped her pack and plopped to the ground before Brin could answer.

Brin looked up from the multimeter. "Really? Uh, I'm almost hungry. Actually, maybe Adam and Kama are . . ." He scanned the hillside. The tube-form dotted the terrain in dense clusters. Each cluster had one or two larger-diameter structures, emerging vertically from the ground and rising just over head-height. Surrounding these were finger-width tangles of tubes, some coiled around each other in tight masses, others branching out into smaller capillary structures before leading back into the soil. The clusters were densest towards the hilltop, and spread out towards the perimeter.

"Hold it . . . oh shit."

"Oh shit, what?" asked Hanid, who was already digging rations out her bag.

"It's an outlier form, six kilometers ahead. I—it's like a gash in the hill and there's . . . something in it . . . it's . . . Hanid, we need to log this."

Hanid sat, suddenly alert. "That form is all solid . . . contiguous. I've never seen a divergence so extreme." She adjusted her visor and scanned the perimeter to the new form. A wide chasm cut up the hill from the distant perimeter to where the pipe-form grew dense towards the top. It shone a dark emerald, as if the hillside was made of sheer glowing crystal with a thin covering of soil and piping. "*Don't* log this. Just look. This is what I meant."

"This is what you *meant*, just look? What are you even talking about?"

"This is how we *witness* it."

"Well, shit! I'm witnessing the biggest outlier form we've ever seen, and Adam and Kama are scouting the interior. Should we wait and see if it expands before sending up a flare for them? What's even protocol for situations like this? *Is* there protocol?"

"Brin, shut up and *look*."

Not knowing what else to do, Brin held fast to his visor, set it to max, and surveyed the chasm. Taken as a whole, it was almost as if the hillside had been sliced clean by scalpel, the walls pulled apart evenly by the tension of the earth's crust. In the magnified scope of Brin's visor, clusters of piping seemed to bend and tumble into the chasm. These edges themselves blurred to an indeterminate fractal gradient. The scope refused to trace the contours of the form and focus drifted almost compulsorily towards the emerald core, from which a sheer chromatic intensity flowed and permeated Brin's sensory field. He pulled away from the scope and rubbed his eyes.

"I can't focus on it, shit. It's not even that bright . . . From here it doesn't look like it's expanding, when you look . . . Hanid?"

Hanid was standing up again, speaking forcefully into a small radio. Brin couldn't hear a sound.

"Hanid . . . what? No transmission in the breach! Right? How did you even get that in? Why are you . . . why can't I hear you?" Brin walked toward her. She pushed him back and continued shouting silently in what Bring perceived to be an unfamiliar language, made up of staccato blasts of hard syllables. He stood aghast. Moments later, she ceased shouting and powered down her radio.

"Sorry, Brin. I—"

"Why couldn't I *hear* you?"

"Yeah, I can explain that, but I need you to listen to me—"

"I'll listen if I can hear you!"

Hanid sighed. "You'll hear me, but *really,* Brin, please. While I talk, I'm going to ask you to keep an eye on the new form, and *don't* look away. Tell me if it's expanding or—"

"I already told you I thought it was!"

"No, you'll know if it is for real. But also if it differentiates."

"How am I gonna take specs on that?"

"No specs! Just watch. This one's off the books, Brin."

Brin scowled into his visor. He let his focus drift and lock into the gleaming field of green.

Hanid proceeded. "As I said, this is how we witness it. The

outlier forms. They change, and that's when it's important. You remember the first time you saw an outlier? In those membrane curtains? They manifested denser than these pipe clusters, and it was like a maze surveying the interior? Four hours in and all of a sudden we started seeing the membranes in braided lattices. At first you wanted to say it was low frequency variation, but I convinced you to log it as an outlier. Remember how I did that?"

"Ah . . . well, you started by making a way better case about *that* than whatever you're on about now."

"No, you just listened better. I told you to look at it and try to follow the strands in the braids. Right?"

"And I couldn't . . . just like this one now."

"Right, because there's indeterminacy at close resolution. It hasn't settled yet, and so there's something happening that we *can't* see. The indeterminacy—how can I say this?—it also reaches *out*. So that's why you can't hear when I broadcast—it's the same output registering on a different band, so to speak."

"Is that how radio interferes with the containment field?"

"That's the theory, actually. It's not so much about the radio transmission itself: containment doesn't involve radio frequencies. But there's some kind of interaction between how the manifest projects indeterminacy and the transmissions. It's like the indeterminacy uses the transmission to step *up* in gain and cancel the containment."

"Hanid . . . how . . . did you work this all out? Is *that* why it's spreading?"

"I told you! If you want to really see It . . . you have *see* It. All these logs—they're not for us, Brin. we can't *see* that kind of data. They're for the Council to run through the network. They think they can do something with it, but they can't. But it was good for a start: whatever's breaching noticed us observing it, and it stabilized. Somewhat. Before it was spinning on its axis and breaching all the fuck over. Now it's in one spot, but I think we need to *keep* noticing it. Intensifying our focus. We witness what it shows us and it shows us more of what it is."

"You're NOT making sense. It's spinning? It's Fast? We're

witnessing? Hanid, all I've ever seen in this breach are dumb, inert shapes out of a demented material science lab that change out of nowhere. You've just illegally transmitted radio waves, weakening breach containment, and you don't answer any of my—"

"But at least you're looking, Brin. And notice how you're *still* looking? That's good . . . there. Now *really see*."

Brin felt a small prick as Hanid pressed a small pen against his neck. It came to Brin as a sudden impact, a pineal thud that rumbled through his organs and dumbed his senses. A field of green came into focus, and receded violently from him in a direction that was neither backward nor forward, but within and in between all other directions. It did not shrink from his vision. Instead it grew larger, even out beyond his visual field. Brin could still see the fractal gradient of the perimeter, but it had ceased to delineate the form of the green chasm from the hillside. It instead acted as a conduit through which the world flowed toward the direction that was nowhere. First the thickets of clustered pipes sped toward the gash's perimeter, unmoored from the soil. Then the soil of the hillside itself, and then Hanid herself, broken and stretched into a thousand spinning iterations as her form followed the infinite course of the fractal cliffs into the green nothingness. Brin was soon to follow.

Nothing but green, but even then it changed. Something twisted from the hidden direction, and behind the green of the breach another form rippled outwards. Ridged black mats shifting atop one another in massive scaled patterns. Shards of sound tumbled out toward Brin and glanced his hearing. The form throbbed and something behind it flexed. Braided ribbon of membranous tissue surged into visibility and stretched taught. Each instance of flexion birthed a new form, better understood as a new aspect of the same vast plane from beyond his perception imprinted on Brin an inescapable sensation of velocity. In the absence of spatial reference, it came to him as a differential tugging through his spine—rapid and directional through his neck and cranium, disintegrating into wisps of motion out through his tailbone. Fast. It was, indeed, moving *quite* fast through his world.

Velocity, yes. But the vector Brin had trouble assessing. It seemed that the more he focused his attention, not on the forms and manifestations themselves, but on the dimensional curvature of their emergence, the more the vector stabilized. It was infinitesimal but perceptible that his awareness was like the dimmest light, a lone speck in a planar void, where even the most insignificant signal shone like a beacon. And it—in its abyssal vastness, was softening its chaotic spinning and orienting toward it. What would happen if more than Hanid and Brin offered their awareness to the mutagenic behemoth that swirled between worlds? What would happen if it began to hurdle, in all speeds, out from the direction that was nowhere, further into their existence? Brin's pulse quickened as he broke his concentration and returned his awareness to the perimeter. Hanid stood where she had moments ago, still in the slack-jawed trance he suspected he had just emerged from. He saw that the pipe-forms had disappeared. The hillside was now cracked with gashes, oozing the neon green light. The nearest crack ran past him and Hanid thirty meters ahead. He scanned it to its termination, which reached almost to the first layer of containment resonators. He was beginning to understand.

Pulpfest 2021

Darrell Schweitzer

I have recently returned from Mars. No, not the planet, the Pittsburgh suburb of Mars, Pennsylvania, which was the site of the 2021 Pulpfest and ERBFest (August 19–21). Admittedly, it felt like Mars the planet at times, or at least the getting there did. To a Philadelphian it seems one cannot possibly make it farther away and still keep it in the state. I also passed through perils on the way, not the meteor swarms that Captain Future dodged with such aplomb, but an Atlantean deluge left over from the remains of Hurricane Fred. It was like driving through a waterfall. I had to wait out the worst of it under an overpass, but I was on high ground then, in the Appalachians (several hundred miles north of John the Balladeer country, but similar), and so was not washed away.

Nevertheless, I arrived at the convention safely and was made welcome. Being welcome was important, because I was going as a dealer, and at least half of the stock I was carrying consisted of my own titles—novels, short story collections, anthologies, and publications I am or have been variously associated with, such as *Weird Tales* and *Weirdbook*. One learns not to take one's "fame" for granted. These folks had to know who I was and give a damn, or else this was going to be a bust. They did. Warm, friendly, interesting people. They spent money freely.

But what does any of this have to do with weird fiction, and why is my own personal frenzy of greed (what behind closed doors in the Star Trek universe is called "a Ferengi orgasm") worth reporting in the pages of the present august journal?

I am getting to that. Pulpfest has a theme (or themes) every year, some of them explicitly focused on weird fiction. H. P. Lovecraft is featured on the cover of the 2015 issue of the convention's impressive annual publication, *The Pulpster* (#24), because one of the themes that year was "Lovecraft at

125." The themes this year might superficially seem less promising—"Romances Pulps at 100" and "The Shadow at 90"—although the lady holding a dainty flower on the cover has a bare skull face and looks suitably eldritch. (The painting is by Graves Gladney, for "Scent of Death," from the *Shadow*, 1 June 1940.)

Programming at Pulpfest is largely of the informational variety. There are a lot of panels elsewhere that consist of people telling stories about themselves or just arguing opinions, but these were carefully planned presentations, usually accompanied by slides or video clips, done by real experts. I learned quite a lot about the Shadow, about whom I had previously known very little: that he began merely as a *shadow* and a voice, a formatting gimmick for radio and short films, not an actual character, but evolved into the familiar avenger with the swirling scarf, slouch hat, and long nose. In some of his earliest incarnations he is hooded and looks more like a mad monk. I also learned a good deal more than I previously knew about love-story pulps (which was close to nothing). These were *the* best-selling pulp category, outselling hero pulps, weird menace, science fiction, westerns, and even general pulps like *Argosy*.

The weird was touched on in a lecture about the leading women pulp editors, because there was much about Dorothy McIlwraith, remembered today mostly as the editor of *Weird Tales* (and a fine one, who developed such writers as Ray Bradbury and Robert Bloch), but in the 1940s regarded as more important for her editorship of *Short Stories,* which was *WT*'s big sister when the two shared the same editor and publisher, and *Short Stories* was a top adventure pulp to rival *Argosy* and *Blue Book*.

Weird Tales artist Margaret Brundage was featured too, during which it was observed (amid many slides) that, despite his popularity, H. P. Lovecraft never got a *WT* cover in his lifetime, probably because he did not care to indulge in the trick, so adeptly mastered by Robert E. Howard and Seabury Quinn, of having nude girls and bondage scenes in his stories. But he *could* have gotten a cover, I suggested from the audience. "The Dreams in the Witch House" was published in the magazine during the Brundage era (1933). As not all Brundage covers faithfully reproduced what was in the stories, we could just see a hideous Brown Jenkin and a younger, sexy, and bare-breasted Keziah Mason descending through the dimensions to terrify the hapless mathematics student. The mind boggles. HPL's mind would have exploded. Maybe it's just as well that this never happened. (I can also imagine a slightly less misleading Brundage cover for "The Thing on the Doorstep" with a nude and seductive Asenath Waite cavorting among the shoggoths.)

I was actually on the program myself, despite my lack of expertise in most topics being addressed, because there were half-hour slots for author readings. I read a suitably *outré* and scary piece called "Killing the Pale Man," about quaint and hideous folk customs in an imaginary part of rural Pennsylvania. This seemed to be well received.

Like any convention, Pulpfest has its own distinct rhythm. This is a daytime convention. Non-locals arrive Wednesday night in order to be there Thursday morning. A buffet breakfast was provided for members in the hotel restaurant, so you tended to get up around 8 A.M. This was the first place to meet and socialize Thursday morning, but the point of all this is dealers' room setup and early-bird shopping. The main activity of Pulpfest is indeed the buying and selling of pulps. The dealers' room is enormous and packed with goodies, ranging from to unique items priced at thousands of dollars down to 1940s western pulps at $3.00 each. I wonder if some of the *Weird Tales* with Conan covers are really worth those four-figure prices put on them. I did not notice any actually selling. (More astonishing in its way: the Girasol *reprint* of the 1932 issue with iconic "batgirl" cover for $250.00.)

I noted that *Weird Tales,* particularly Howard or Lovecraft issues, continue to soar into the hundreds of dollars per copy. The time to have collected these was at least a generation ago. Prices on *Unknown* and pulp-sized *Astounding* are dropping. You could get a lot of B-grade copies in the teens of dollars, sometimes even less. It may be that these are just too common, as they are assiduously preserved by generations of collectors who are now dying off, or it may be that people are not collecting the Campbell-era writers (even Heinlein) the way they are collecting the Farnsworth Wright–era writers.

Most unique item in the dealers' room: a leather-bound, *signed* copy of Edgar Rice Burroughs fandom's most legendary samizdat, the entirely illegal and never-to-be-published *Tarzan on Mars* by "John Bloodstone," a.k.a. S. J. Byrne, apparently the author's own copy, for $600. Most unlikely encounter: While I was chatting with Chet Williamson, whose table was perpendicular to mine, a lady looked at the pulps spread out on Chet's table, then showed us some pictures of some very rare issues of *All-Story,* asking if we had any of them. It turned out that she was the great-granddaughter of the woman who posed for the original *Thuvia, Maid of Mars* cover in 1916.

There were also a lot of new books, specially published for the pulp market, reprints of pulp fiction, magazine facsimiles, and anthologies. I saw the new, revised edition of *The Weird Tales Story* (by Robert Weinberg, and now et al.) for the first time, noting that my name is on the table of contents six times. (My own copies are still in transit as I write this.) Will Murray had a whole table of his varied products. I was not alone selling my own titles. He is a better fit for Pulpfest and was one of the major guests, since he is a one-man neo-pulp industry, churning out new Doc Savage and (authorized) Tarzan material. I had brought along my copy of *King Kong vs. Tarzan* for him to sign and also picked up his new *Tarzan, Conqueror of Mars*. (Sorry, Will. I just never got into Doc Savage.)

I regret that I missed Will Murray's own presentation, since it was during dealer-room hours and I was much too busy relieving people of their cash. Fortunately, a lot of the best programming was in the evening, after which people either hung out in the lounge/bar area, watched the film program (Shadow movies, most of them more of curio value than merit). Also in the evening there was a presentation of the Munsey Award for services to the pulp field, which went to Rich Harvey, for Bold Venture Press and for his organizing of the smaller but more frequent Pulp Adventurecons. At the Saturday night auctions, many things (including some Arkham House books) went surprisingly cheaply, though they did get around $700 for Walter Gibson's typewriter. I suspect this was one of Gibson's later typewriters, not the one he wrote his 1930s pulp novels on. It looked like a 1960s model.

The last thing Saturday night was the Barsoomian Bull Session, which went fairly late. Sunday morning at Pulpfest is for last-minute bargain shopping. I found such bargains, particularly from one dealer whose pulps were, quite frankly, overpriced. He had apparently done badly, but Sunday morning he marked everything down to $5, at which point the vultures descended.

A wonderful convention. I intend to return.

The Weird Elegance of Molly Tanzer's Early Fiction

Javier Martinez

MOLLY TANZER. *A Pretty Mouth*. Petaluma, CA: Word Horde Press, 2021. 270 pp. $17.99 tpb. ISBN: 9781939905628
MOLLY TANZER. *Rumbullion*. Petaluma, CA: Word Horde Press, 2021. 156 pp. $17.99 tpb. ISBN: 9781939905642
MOLLY TANZER. *The Pleasure Merchant*. Petaluma, CA: Word Horde Press, 2021. 349 pp. $17.99 tpb. ISBN: 9781939905666

For the last decade or so, Molly Tanzer has published a considerable body of elegant writing that is characterized by a variety of disparate, even contradicting, influences. Lovecraftian gods mix with parlor drama; body horror plays against a backdrop of the novel of manners; sensual erotica embraces sardonic humor. Tanzer is adept at juggling all these things and more in stories and novels that are intensely readable, literary, and always subversive in their narrative development and in their political implications. Her work is populated by characters historically relegated to the margins—people of color play prominent roles, as do folks from the LGBTQ community—and traditional historical narratives are disrupted by queer and complex retellings. If only for these reasons, it is valuable to have these Word Horde Press reissued versions of Tanzer's early work: *A Pretty Mouth,* originally published by LFP in 2012; *Rumbullion,* originally published in 2013 as part of the collection *Rumbullion and Other Liminal Libations* by Egaeus Press and as a standalone *Rumbullion: An Apostrophe* by LFP in 2016; and *The Pleasure Merchant,* originally published in 2016 by LFP. All these are the author's preferred editions and as such serve as the perfect portal for new readers and as opportunities—at least in the case of *The Pleasure Merchant,* which Tanzer refers to on her website as the "extremely preferred" edition—for those familiar with Tanzer's work to revisit her early writings.

In her introduction to the new edition of *A Pretty Mouth*, Tanzer asks herself and her readers if her first book is a "collection, a mosaic novel or something else entirely?" One is tempted to respond with an all-encompassing "Yes," for what we have is Tanzer's attempt, prompted by her editor and publisher the bizarro author Cameron Pierce, to expand her original story "An Infernal History of the Ivybridge Twins" (included here as the third story in the collection) into a full-fledged novel. Rather than expanding that story, Tanzer instead opted to flesh out the sordid and uncanny familial history of that story's main characters, the Calabash twins, over a series of five complementary stories, including "A Spotted Trouble at Dolor-on-the-Downs," "The Hour of the Tortoise," the aforementioned "Ivybridge Twins," "A Pretty Mouth," and "Damnatio Memoriae." The stories are presented in reverse chronological order, beginning in the late nineteenth or early twentieth century with "A Spotted Trouble," a Wodehouse-inspired Jeeves story that features a Lovecraftian selkie. "Tortoise" takes us back a century or so and is more overtly Lovecraftian for its Outsider-like main character (in tone, if not in body) and, perhaps, for its delineation of frustrated homosexual desire. "Ivybridge Twins" reads like an eighteenth-century account of the body-swapping anxiety in "The Whisperer in Darkness," but it owes just as much to the British Boarding School story tradition, with the type of gender-appropriate twists one would expect from Tanzer. The titular "A Pretty Mouth," taking place during the Restoration period, makes overt the class tensions of the British Boarding School story and infuses them with a more sinister revenge narrative coupled, again, with frustrated homosexual need. The closing story, "Damnatio Memoriae," reframes the entire narrative, documenting the curse that is visited upon the noble Roman progenitor of the Calabash clan, effectively infusing a dose of the tragic into their decadence and corruption and complicating readers' judgment of all that has come before (or will come after).

Tanzer is too hard on herself and on these stories in her introduction to *A Pretty Mouth*. She writes, "It's been a long near-decade and I'm not sure I understand the person who wrote these stories, and I'm not sure if I did at the time, either." While she goes on to say that the stories "still slap," she also points out that they "contain errors" of "pacing, errors of tone; errors I have tried to correct as I revisited these stories for this new edition, and errors I let stand for one reason or another." Most tellingly, she writes that "given some of the more outré themes herein, this is both an introduction and content warning . . . given how different *A Pretty Mouth* is from my more recent work. In its treatment of sex and sexuality, of gender and identity, of morality and violence, I figured I'd caution any reader who might be coming to this after reading, for example, *Creatures of Will and Temper* (2017)." But no reader who enjoys literary, elegant prose and a solid grasp of storytelling conventions, and how those conventions can be upended, need be concerned. Tanzer's self-deprecations aside, she also points out that she is "extremely proud of this book and what [she] accomplished with it." And well she should be. This new edition of *A Pretty Mouth* provides readers a polished look at a unique writer at the beginning of her career.

While *A Pretty Mouth* opens with a quotation for Henry Fielding's picaresque work from 1749, *Tom Jones,* it is *Rumbullion* and *The Pleasure Merchant* that best embody the characteristics of the eighteenth-century English novel. In her introduction to *Rumbullion,* Tanzer describes the novella as "Rashomon with fops"—an apt and accurate a description as any—and as representative of her "favorite sort of story to write. There's an anxious frame containing lots of little bits and bobs—a letter, a script, a confession. I especially enjoy the epistolary mode, and its potential to succinctly suggest a bigger world and a larger story." At approximately 140 pages, *Rumbullion* manages all these "bits and bobs" that Tanzer describes, even as it unravels, quite unexpectedly but most deftly, a neatly done horror twist in the closing pages. The novella is presented as a series of letters and journal entries, mostly from the perspective of Julian Bretwynde as he attempts to determine the nature of the events that occurred at a party that degenerated into a bacchanalian spectacle and murder. Echoes of

Machen's *The Great God Pan* can be found throughout, but maintain a subtle distance so as not to obscure more than necessary the multiple and at time conflicting perspectives that Julian tries to make sense of. One of these perspectives comes from the Count of Saint Germain, but that historic person's sinister reputation is eclipsed by another of the party's attendees by story's end. A kind of parlor mystery, the narrative progression of *Rumbullion* satisfies the needs of the mystery reader, slowly illuminating the events of the party, introducing and gradually developing the confusing occurrences, and finally revealing the mystery at the heart of things even as the reveal points to larger, barely glimpsed horror. According to the Oxford University Press Blog, the word *rumbullion* means "a great tumult" and was adopted by Devonshire settlers in the Caribbean, which plays a distant but important role in the story. "A great tumult" is an accurate way of describing the events in the novella, and its root "rum" points not only to the intoxicatory effects of the alcohol and drugs used at the party, but to the altered state of consciousness induced in the partygoers from an obscure supernatural source. It is this source that offers a satisfying glimpse of "a bigger world and larger story," which is at least partly reintroduced in Tanzer's 2015 novel *Vermillion*.

Rumbullion very neatly prefigures the languid splendor and decorous prose of Tanzer's recent Diabolist Library trilogy (2017–20), but also her other Word Horde Press reissue, the novel *The Pleasure Merchant*. The story charts the rise and fall of Tom Dawne, apprentice wig-maker, who is guided through a secret London social scene by his desire to advance his social station on the one hand, and his loins on the other. He is most taken by Miss Tabula Rassa, who unbeknownst to Tom is an apprentice pleasure merchant, or someone who is hired to make real the secret dreams and desires of those who can afford their services. More than a high-class prostitute, however, Tabula is self-sufficient, well-educated, and adept at navigating any number of social circles. While Tom is the central character of the novel, it is Tabula who is the heart of the story. Her name speaks to her unknown past, which of course is gradually revealed over the course of the novel. There are fantastical elements in play, too, specifically a type of mesmerism that holds many of the book's characters in thrall to the naturally unlikable antagonist of the story. The parlor-room mystery in *Rumbullion* is amplified here to include the entirety of London, and there is real delight to be had in reading Tanzer's rich evocation of the literary city, if not the actual one. While formulaic—Tom gets his just deserts, the villain gets his comeuppance, Tabula learns who she really is, and those who deserve a happy ending receive their reward—the novel is also innovative in its use of multiple points of view; its use of first-, second-, and third-person voice; its use of letters, journal entries, and its direct address to the reader. The novel's greatest strength is how it deploys Tanzer's bold narrative techniques in the guise of a traditional story told well.

Tanzer refers to this work as a novel of "desire and dismay," and that serves not only as a description of the novel, but of the author's experience writing and revising it for this edition. In her introduction Tanzer describes her reaction to the final draft of the original, pre-revised novel: "I'd ended up with a novel that felt baroque, but not in the way I'd hoped. As I edited the manuscript, it only got bigger, every sentence a hydra." As is often the case with writers' judging the quality of their work, others disagreed: "My agent liked it, my editor liked it, my beta reader liked it. Maybe I was wrong? What did I know?" Upon revisiting the novel five years later to prepare it for this current edition, Tanzer realizes that she "hadn't trusted [the] reader. The book was overwritten, stuffed with the unnecessary. I'd beaten [the] readers over the head with every beat, every emotion, every connection, every detail." This "extremely preferred" current version contains approximately thirteen percent less text that the original, but Tanzer informs us that she did not cut a single scene, but instead "pruned around them." The excised material, Tanzer tells us, was extraneous information about eighteenth-century English culture that got in the way of the story. Aside from the insight that Tanzer provides into her editing process, what strikes me as especially relevant here is how she channels her love of the Restoration period into her fiction. This more streamlined version is thus Tanzer's attempt to impart in subtle and organic ways the narrative tone and textual feel of eighteenth-century English fiction. This reflective and reflexive exercise points to Tanzer's maturation as a writer and as a creative artist who can exert control over her work. Indeed, her prose is polished and honed, her pacing steady, and her story engaging. In other words, all the best aspects of the classic English novel are packaged and redeployed in a story that also incorporates our contemporary interests with ethnic diversity and gender fluidity. To borrow a phrase from the science fiction critic John Reider, Tanzer's stories make explicit what is mostly implicit in eighteenth-century English fiction.

On a closing note—and aside from the literary qualities of these books, of which there are many— one would be remiss not to point out the handsome packaging of these new editions. Australian designer Matthew Revert is as adept at recreating scenes from eighteenth-century English life as he is at designing seedy grindhouse packaging that seems to have come to us straight from the pop culture dregs of the '70s and '80s. It is truly lovely work that Revert has done for Word Horde Press's Molly Tanzer Collection and is yet another reason for readers of the weird to search out these fine works.

A Beautiful Bouquet

Dave Felton

DANIEL MILLS. *Among the Lilies*. Pickering, ON: Undertow Publications, 2021. 260 pp. $17.99 tpb. ISBN 9781988964317.

"I am tired of ghost stories," Daniel Mills begins in his latest collection of weird fiction, *Among the Lilies*. It is a curious statement to make when that is what readers have come to want from an author walking in the footsteps of Hawthorne, Poe, and Lovecraft. With two novels—*Revenants* (Chomu Press, 2011), set in colonial New England, and *Moriah* (ChiZine, 2017), set in nineteenth-century Vermont—and the collection *The Lord Came at Twilight* (Dark Renaissance, 2014), Mills has staked out the early years of America to weave tales of Gothic fiction and, yes, ghost stories. "They are always the same," he continues in the opening lines of "Below the Falls," the first story. "A respectable narrator visits a country house where he experiences a series of unsettling incidents before the final appearance of the ghost bursts on his mind like a thunderclap. His faith is shattered or his sanity. He is changed forever." While this formula of shattered faith and broken sanity is certainly true for many writers of horror, even masters such as Lovecraft and Robert W. Chambers, there are points where Mills diverges from the path of those who came before him, and such divergences circumvent hackneyed pitfalls of the genre.

In the twelve stories of *Among the Lilies,* the reader will certainly find the horrific—crawling corpses, paranormal events, witches in woods, murder, and ghosts—but tying these together are unmistakable bonds of family relationships: parents, siblings, grandparents, aunts and uncles, spouses, children. The ways these familial bonds are subverted, broken, or altogether absent cause characters mental and physical distress that manifest in tragedy. In "Below the Falls," an eighteen-year-old girl is traumatized by her father's suicide and sexual assault by her stepfather, only to be later institutionalized by a controlling husband. The main character in "The Woman in the Wood" is a fifteen-year-old mentally ill boy sent to stay with his uncle and pregnant aunt who "stinks of sin"; he writes his obscene nightmares in a notebook either to record or to exorcize them, only to see them played out in the natural world. In another piece, "Lucilla Barton (1857–1880)," a family tragedy unfolds through a series of public records, newspaper articles, and court testimonies; there are suggestions of a witch's curse that follows the birth of a child, but those afflicted or haunted are dismissed as drunk or insane. In these stories the act of childbirth is often seen as shameful and perverse, infants as things to be hidden or buried, and religion holds no comfort, used only to pervert the natural order and control the minds of the faithful.

Some of the material in this volume has appeared elsewhere in themed anthologies and bear the mark of their intent. For example, "A Shadow Passing," published in *Autumn Cthulhu* by the Lovecraft eZine Press in 2016, uses details of Lovecraft's life to reimagine or refashion him as a boy just days after the Old Gent's actual death in 1937. It is Lovecraft yet not Lovecraft, recognizable to all who know of his early life in Providence: a sickly child, an insane mother, a doting aunt, a distant grandfather and his books, a church on a hill. This cleverly rearranges the familiar to make it new for fans, but may not translate as well for readers unversed in Lovecraft's biography. On the other hand, the story "The Lake," which first appeared in *Aickman's Heirs* (Undertow Publications, 2015), unfolds so transparently and effortlessly as a coming-of-age ghost story that there's little trace of the author's hand or inspiration.

"The Account of David Stonehouse, Exile," originally published as a limited-edition chapbook by Dim Shores Press and long out of print, is the longest piece of this collection. It is a tale of survival, a solitary man eking out an existence in an untamed wilderness of unforgiving elements, savage wolves, and a vengeful ghost, with only a skittish dog by his side. Mills conjures such primitive conflict in sparse direct language, much like Hemingway in similar tales of outdoorsmanship, and it suits the mood and character. "I thought of nothing, or rather, would not think, would not let myself remember," Stonehouse writes in his journal. He saves his attention for tracking moose, trapping squirrels, and fishing in a nearby creek, where he pulls out the decayed body of a fallen soldier. "I became someone else," he realizes. "I hunted game with the soldier's rifle and wore his coat. Afterward I warmed my hands at another man's stove and slept in the blankets his family left behind. Even this book is his, not mine." The protagonist lapses into reverie with increasing frequency, recalling his years in the religious community that raised him and groomed him for divine revelation through dream interpretation. There is a Puritan feel to "the Village," but it is left as an archetypal sect, a cult with no tolerance for illicit love, with the power to cast transgressors out into the wilderness. In these moments Stonehouse takes on the role of the biblical Cain, scorned by God's chosen and forsaken to wander the earth. In Mills's world, it is an earth where spirits are restless, the dead walk again and ride upon the backs of wolves among tall pines whose roots nourish—and are nourished by—corpses.

The strongest story in this collection is "Lilies," a romance in the tradition of the Brontës and Henry James that was first published in 2012 and now appears in an extensively rewritten form. A young man, orphaned at an early age, sets out to visit a reclusive uncle in Maine and befriends a pair of siblings on the train ride. Unsurprisingly, he falls in love with the sister while the brother is opposed to the affair, an almost necessary conflict in the gothic tale. The dialogue between these three, from playful banter to touching declarations, is unseen elsewhere in the book and reveals the author's skill and attention to characterization. As master of Bittersweet Lodge, Uncle Edward works obsessively on ancient historical texts under the portrait of his wife, dead for forty-four years, believed to have fallen ill due to the restless spirit of Lily Stark, a young woman who had previously died in the house and was buried in unconsecrated ground on the estate. Her spirit is feared to haunt the property and harm any other woman who makes it her home. "Lily is not at rest," Uncle Edward tells his nephew. "She is as much a part of this house as the bittersweet vines she planted. Her presence pervades this house, her ago-ny. The desperation of her final moments. Her rage. That, above all." The optimism of young love hopes to prevail, and the restoration of Lily Stark's forgotten grave to a place of beauty is thought to break her hold on the estate, but illness and death always reassert their power in the end.

Like most titles by Undertow Publications, Daniel Mills's *Among the Lilies* is a thing of beauty, designed by Vince Haig and adorned with cover art by Yves Tourigny. Tourigny's stylized illustration captures the feel of a nineteenth-century landscape engraving, presumably depicting the untamed woods of New England. Upon finishing the collection, a closer look reveals it to be a scene from "The Account of David Stonehouse, Exile," with a pack of wolves under three pines; and here, a final tease of Mills's smooth writing: "Three trees tall as ship's masts and acres of empty forest spread round, the soil barren with needles and undercut by pine-roots. It is a place for the dead, as is the whole of this valley, where no living crops grow." A place for the dead, indeed, but also for the imagination, as Daniel Mills welcomes readers through his dark woods, dreaded hills, and lonely shores. Whether the horror is the supernatural infringing upon mortal senses or the broken minds of people pushed beyond their tolerance for pain, the stories in *Among the Lilies* are full of hauntings that feel both familiar and real, and are well worth seeking out.

Finally, Support for a New Type of Slasher Story

June Pulliam

GRADY HENDRIX. *The Final Girls Support Group.* New York: Berkley Publishing, 2021. 352 pp. $26.00 hc. ISBN: 978-0593201237.

The slasher film genre operates by its own set of rules: a faceless (and usually male) killer murders several young women, each kill more horrific than the next, until one of the women stops him and survives to emerge as the Final Girl, slayer of monsters (at least until the next sequel in her franchise), and the credits roll. Slasher films are a sort of Grand Guignol of patriarchal cautionary tales for women: if you want to live, don't have sex, don't drink or do drugs, be a conscientious babysitter, pay attention to your surroundings at all times. Failing to adhere to these rules means that you're asking for it, sister. But also, don't expect that these rules constitute any sort of contract that will prevent you from being targeted by the slasher or having to fight all over again in the sequel. No one knows this better than Laurie Strode (Jamie Lee Curtis) of the *Halloween* franchise, who is now fighting off Michael Myers with her daughter and granddaughter. Yet even intra-generational sisterhood is inadequate for making the world safe again from Michael Myers or the systematic oppression of women through the threat of violence, because being aware of the rules of the narrative is not enough to change them in the world of the slasher film.

Grady Hendrix's slasher novel *The Final Girl Support Group,* however, does consider what is necessary to change not just the reality of the slasher film, but the world where an entire genre of film where women are terrorized and killed is blockbuster entertainment. And the short answer is not some version of the Video Nasties laws.

Like the newest installments in the *Halloween* franchise, *The Final Girl Support Group* considers the fate of the final girl character long after her ordeal is over. For Hendrix's protagonist Lynette and the other final girls she knows, being a final girl is a transformative experience. You don't just hand off your crown to the next final girl as if you are Miss America at the end of her year. Instead, final girls are trapped in their identities by PTSD, which causes them to be hypervigilant, self-destructive, and unable to trust anyone else fully (individual results may vary).

Hendrix's final girls are more than just one-dimensional characters in most slasher films. They are women whose girlhood ended the moment that their would-be killers slaughtered their friends and family as they watched. These women's identities are even further reduced after someone capitalizes on their ordeals to create successful slasher film franchises whose final girls are their better-known analogues. Perhaps this is why Adrienne is the first to die in the present day of *TFGSG:* the only woman of color whose experience inspired a popular slasher film franchise, Adrienne successfully sued the franchise's producers for what amounts to copyright infringement for their unauthorized use of her life story, enjoining them from creating any more sequels as well as seizing their profits. Adrienne uses this money to purchase Camp Red Lake, the place where she unwittingly became a final girl, and turns it into a retreat for victims of violence, then reboots the franchise based on her ordeal to finance this center. In this way, Adrienne took control franchise's distorted narrative of her life (where the producers cast her as white) to help other survivors resist attempts to contort and reduce their stories into victim status. After Adrienne's murder, Lynette realizes that someone is coming for her sister survivors as well, and living requires more than just being armed with the best weapons, hunkering down within a fortified shelter, or being guarded by a private army.

In what turns out to be Lynette's last group therapy session, Hendrix shows how this group is more divided by petty differences than united by what they have in common. Bitchiness and backbiting among the women in the group undermine their collective ability to do more than just support one another. This cattiness is exhibited when the other members of the group turn in Lynette and tell her that she is not a "real" final girl because all she did was survive after someone slaughtered her baby sister, her boyfriend, and her parents in front of her. Instead of fighting off her would-be killer, Lynette merely did not expire after he impaled her on a deer's antlers mounted in her family home and left her for dead. That any member of the Final Girl Support Group would even make such a distinction between "real" and "fake" final girl indicates how their thinking has been co-opted by the language of the slasher film. The group members' cattiness is not the natural consequence of being female, but rather the result of deep gender programming that is much older than the slasher genre. This programming is part of a sweeping cultural narrative that teaches women to view one another as competitors for the dubious prize of male adoration rather than as allies who can resist this narrative and collaborate to overthrow a dominator model of society.

After Adrienne's murder, Lynette is targeted by the same killer, and she fights back by seeking out her sister final girls to unmask him. When Lynette finds her would-be murderer after multiple plot twists, she declines to become a "real" final girl by killing him. Instead, she chooses to let him live and go to prison where he will have time to "see just how small and meaningless [his] murders were." By resisting the script, Lynette can exit the story of the slasher film, where the victims are "reduced to splatter effects who only got first names" as well as help others resist the internalized programming that divides people into virgins and victims, predators and prey so they can be the protagonists of their own stories.

The Unnamed and the Unnamable

Hank Wagner

MICHAEL SHEA. *Mr. Cannyharme: A Novel of Lovecraftian Terror.* Edited by S. T. Joshi. New York: Hippocampus Press, 2021. 300 pp. $45.00 limited cloth, ISBN 9781614983255; $20.00 tpb. ISBN 9781614983248; $6.00 ebook, ISBN 9781614983262.

Edited by noted Lovecraft scholar S. T. Joshi, *Mr. Cannyharme* brings to light a manuscript from some four decades old, left by the late, great Michael Shea, telling the stories of several down-on-their-luck denizens of a seedy San Francisco Mission District hotel, known as The Hyperion, who find themselves facing a supernatural threat that has lived silently in their midst for decades. That threat is represented in corporeal form by longtime resident of the establishment, the ancient, vaguely threatening Mr. Cunningham. Unknown to them, Cunningham has dastardly, self-serving plans for many of his neighbors; whether they succumb to his evil machinations or find it within themselves to resist depends largely on their free will, the strength of their characters, and their innate sense of self.

Fans of the Hugo, Nebula, Locus, and World Fantasy nominee will instantly fall in love with this recently uncovered, lovingly restored treasure; those unfamiliar with his work until now will likely see it as a gateway to Shea's very worthy backlist, which includes novels like *Nifft the Lean* (1982) and *In Yana, the Touch of the Undying* (1985), and the short story collections *Polyphemus* (1987) and *The Autopsy and Other Tales* (2008). Springing from H. P. Lovecraft's seminal short story, "The Hound" (famous for the first mention of that infamous Book of the Dead, the *Necronomicon*), it deftly explores themes prevalent in both Lovecraft's and Shea's other works. Further drawing on from Lovecraft's depressing oeuvre (which Shea successfully accessed many times over his career, in novels like

The Colour out of Time [1984] and in the 2009 short story collection *Copping Squid and Other Mythos Tales*), it warns of malevolent forces waiting to prey on the unsuspecting, and of the thin, gossamer curtain separating the real and unreal, the everyday and the cosmic. From Shea's perspective, it illustrates both the frailty and nobility of humanity, showing the tendency to succumb to weakness and addiction, but also the ability to transcend tragedy and move through life, despite its many challenges. Building toward, and culminating with, a bizarre banquet, as memorable and terrifying as the feast at the center of Edgar Allan Poe's "The Masque of the Red Death," hosted by none other than the terrifying Mr. Cunningham, and facilitated by his macabre minions, it is a story that simultaneously fills its readers with hope and despair.

A World of One

Géza A. G. Reilly

MICHAEL CISCO. *Antisocieties*. New Orleans: Grimscribe Press, 2021. 154 pp. $20.00 tpb. ISBN: 9780578836881.

What would an "antisociety" look like? I'm tempted to apprehend the term in two ways. In one, I envision it as "anti-society," or the quality of a person who is against society writ large. In the other, I envision it as "anti society," or a potential term for a society that is focused on negation—even negation of itself. How could such a society function? Who would be its members? Could it sustain a population of more than one? To a large degree, I came away from Michael Cisco's *Antisocieties* without any more clarity on the matter than I had going in. However, while I think that Cisco doesn't quite straddle the two worlds of horror fiction and experimental fiction as well as possible, I can give credit to him for at least grappling with how the uncompromising citizens of antisocieties would live.

This was my first experience of Cisco's writing, insofar as I can remember, and it was an interesting way to dive into his work. There is a lot of skill and craft in this collection of short stories, though I admit that I felt the whole of *Antisocieties* was less than satisfying. Perhaps that is understandable for a collection of this nature, which is (according to the publisher's blurb) "ten stories about isolation—what it does to people, and what isolated people do to each other and themselves. [. . .] A succession of portraits of people trapped in their own identities, some of whom insist on their own ideas because they would have nothing at all without them." As blurbs go, this is certainly an arresting one for a man of a certain temperament like me! All the same, I found that not many of the stories in this collection lived up to the promise.

Let's clear the ground with a discussion of the stories that resonated with me and why, for there is much to enjoy in Cisco's narratives. Two stood out immediately in my first reading: "Saccade" and "Water Machine." These stories are some of the least opaque in the collection, in terms of plot, and are also two of the strangest works present. "Saccade" is a mind-bending tale about the nuances of sight, language, and facts of existence that would be better left unknown to humanity. "Water Machine" is a truly bizarre story about a doctor treating an institutionalized schizophrenic with some all-too-fascinating theories about mathematics, language, and evolution. Both of these stories were highlights of the collection for me because they were entirely contained, reasonably understandable, and fiercely dark narratives.

Others were almost as strong. The eponymous "Antisocieties," for example, was a Kafkaesque story about an administrator coming to visit a man who is seemingly kept in what I can only describe as a mundane-appearing garden of people. A tragedy, almost a *conte cruel,* the tale has a strong anti-authoritarian air to it—but anti-authoritarian in the sense that one should be willing to hurl oneself at an overly imposing brick wall over and over again. "Stillville" reminded me of a heretofore unknown text by Thomas Ligotti. The story—almost a series of prose poems—focuses on the trials of a man who works in one town but lives in another. The trick is that the town in which he lives is bereft of motion, as though the only force present is inertia itself. Finally, "The Starving of Saqqara" starts as a near-homage to pulp fiction, with the narrator discovering and then researching a compelling (and inherently contradictory) limestone sculpture that he happens upon in a museum. However, the story unravels a bit toward the end, and it ultimately left me wondering what exactly had happened—and more importantly, *why*.

This is an ongoing issue of mine with a good amount of ostensible horror fiction. I don't expect narratives to be easy to read or clearly possessed of a traditional structure, but I do prefer stories that have *some* sort of hook for readers to grasp onto and use to make sense of what they are reading. Truly chaotic, purposeless horror fictions are possible, but they are rare, and they take the hand of someone like Robert Aickman to produce. Many of the stories in *Antisocieties* left me struggling to determine the meaning within, and that is why, for me, the collection as a whole doesn't quite work. The collection's opener, "Intentionally Left Blank," for example, is the story of a young man encountering a person or being that is more of a void made manifest than anything else. He is, in a sense, a signifier without a signified—he is the "blank" of the title, as it were. This is an idea with a lot of legs to it (since it is the Halloween season, I would be remiss if I were not to point out the obvious connection to Michael Myers—the Shape—in the film *Halloween*), but here it lands with more than a bit of a thud. The story is finely written, certainly, but there is no kind of why or how that readers can catch in order to understand the occurrences within the story. What readers are left with, instead, is the vague notion that a person impossibly devoid of identity is somehow infectious and can inexplicably cause one person (out of many who have encountered the "blank" person to no ill effect) to lose his identity.

To return to the dual image that opened this review, if each of these stories deals with an anti society, a society centered paradoxically on isolation and negation rather than community and identity, then Cisco has embarked on an intriguing project that almost hits the mark but, for me, just falls short. The ideas in this collection are fascinating when they are articulated in such a way that readers can understand them, but they often don't have enough of the meat of a *story* to make them satisfying. Cisco's prose is wonderful throughout, there's no denying that, and he is often able to unsettle the reader with the most innocuous of phrases. I'll certainly be seeking out more of his work listed on the back of this collection. But *Antisocieties,* taken as a whole, seems to have one foot in the world of horror fiction and one foot in the world of experimental fiction, and ultimately, it cannot maintain the balance it needs to thrive in both realms. Perhaps it is ironic that I'm criticizing *Antisocieties* for having so much trouble with maintaining a literary identity, and perhaps others will see more in the collection than I have been able to discern; but for me the collection remains an intriguing, often beautiful, but unfortunately failed compromise.

Delving into Darkness

Darrell Schweitzer

LISA TUTTLE. *The Dead Hours of Night*. Richmond, VA: Valancourt Books, 2021. 234 pp. $16.99 tpb. ISBN 9781948405836.

I confess I have been following Lisa Tuttle's fiction for a very long time indeed. We were in fanzine fandom at the same time, in the late 1960s, and I received her 'zine *Mathom*. I remember her very first story, which was about a kid hatched out of an Easter egg, and I published a couple more of hers in my *Procrastination*. A *lot* of water has gone under the proverbial bridge since then, and in the meantime Tuttle matured into a master of the rich and strange. She collaborated with George R. R. Martin on *Windhaven*. She has written numerous very fine novels on her own, including *The Pillow Friend, The Mysteries, The Silver Bough*, etc. She is also one of the preeminent ghost story or "strange story" (to use Robert Aickman's term) writers of our time, someone whose work you would put on the same shelf with Aickman, or perhaps Thomas Ligotti.

Readers of this new collection will note all the usual excellences: the measured prose, the subtle use of detail, characters that live and have complex lives; but you will also note how *physical* many of these stories are, often a low-key version of what has been called "body horror," almost as if Shirley Jackson had collaborated with Clive Barker. For example, in "A Birthday," a young man is distressed to see that his mother (whom he does not visit often) seems to be bleeding copiously, even though she says she is fine and shows no sign of weakness. The female body may be a mystery to young men, but this is clearly wrong, out of the ordinary, even if nobody else seems to agree. Did he imagine the whole thing? His mother is found to have collapsed into a bloody mass, and there's a newborn baby. The young man is congratulated as the father. Nightmare? Incest?

In "My Pathology" an alchemist is growing the philosopher's stone inside cancerous tumors in a woman's body. In "Food Man," a young girl is deliberately starving herself, not only out of an obsession with body image, but because she feels a sense of power doing it. She dumps food under her bed until the rotting mass comes to life in the form of a foul-smelling man, with whom she has a sexual relationship. In "Born Dead" a career woman takes over the care of a child that was born dead; yet the body continues to grow into adulthood. This proves to be all too convenient, given her life and plans. The story ends with a bit of Jane Austen-ish snark: "Reader, I married him."

In the one period piece, "Mr. Elphinstone's Hands," a nineteenth-century medium who exudes ectoplasm gives his gift to a woman. It's a sticky mess, very physical, even as he tries to manifest himself through it.

One of the very darkest is "Closet Dreams," about a girl who suffers what is very close to the ultimate horror, being kidnapped, kept in a closet, and continuously raped. She escapes and survives to adulthood, but her escape is so implausible, so inexplicable, that she is in the nightmare situation of doubting it really happened.

This is indeed strong stuff. It would have given M. R. James a fit, if not a heart attack, though before he succumbed he might have been able to admire the technique, which in many ways, despite the subject matter, is that of the classic ghost story. Little hints of wrongness in ordinary life, until by the end of the story the wrongness is front and center. Not all these stories are 100% successful. The weakest one is, surprisingly, the one from the classic 1980 anthology *Dark Forces*. "Where the Stones Grow" has creepy moments, but ultimately it is a "man encounters the supernatural, then he dies" story, in which the character unknowingly goes to his doom without having done any wrong, or gained any terrible insight other than "don't mess with haunted stones." "The Dream Detective" is a fine story as it stands, about a woman who "solves" crimes that happen in dreams and then is murdered in a dream. Her body is still alive, but her soul seems gone. Where she once refused to sensationalize, much less commercially exploit her "gift," she now becomes crassly commercial, has a bestselling book, and is soon to have a TV show. Yet when the "murderer" has her autograph a book at a book-signing, she writes in it, "Save me." Now, is that an ending, or the end of chapter 1? It leaves us with a chill, but it also could lead to something much larger. He plight is unresolved. The "murderer's" guilt is unresolved. This could have made an interesting novel. Maybe it still can.

In any case, *The Dead Hours of Night* will give you hours of disquieting entertainment. Not for the squeamish.

Achieving That Rare Alchemy

The joey Zone

ROY V. HUNT. *A Retrospective*. Edited by David and Daniel Ritter. Cambridge, MA: First Fandom Experience, 2021. 144 pp. $45.00 tpb. ISBN: 9781733296465.

1.

I gave posthumous thanks to Leah Bodine Drake in my review of her recent Hippocampus omnibus collection two issues ago in this journal. She made me aware of Denver Colorado's Roy Vernon Hunt (1914–1986) through her review of fellow Denver Scientifiction fan, writer, and publisher Stanley Mullen's *Moonfoam and Sorceries* (Gorgon Press, 1948). Happily, thanks to David and Daniel Ritter and First Fandom Experience (firstfandomexperience.org), gratitude may be extended while contemporaneous.

FFE has published *The Visual History of Science Fiction Fandom, Volume One: The 1930s*, an expensive but essential reference work. This organization is doing important research, giving Credit Where Due to all us fans, Past, Present and Future, from nascent talents cultivating art or writing up to Dirty Old Pros. Although decrying this collection of Hunt's as "not fully comprehensive," one is hard put to imagine any volume possibly more engaging or worthy of being on a shelf next to similar collections of Bok or Finlay.

The reproductions in this artist's monograph are impeccable, from the restoration of faint empurpled mimeographed fanzines to white gouache stipple (*Voice of the Imagi-Nation* and *Fantasy Advertiser* covers). There is a ten-page section describing the various technologies used to produce early fanzines, from offset lithography down to hectography, while a four-page chronological index of work featuring Hunt's art rounds out the text.

Illustration from *The Alchemist* 1, No. 3 (Summer 1940). Roy V. Hunt channels the influence of Lynd Ward in this woodblock print.

2.

In *The Alchemist* 1, No. 1 (February 1940), the young fan Roy Hunt gave one of the earliest reviews of H. P. Lovecraft's *The Outsider and Others*. One might say it was somewhat positive:

> it is the most outstanding volume of bizarre classics to be published . . . You will entirely forget that you are reading printed pages as you are swept completely into the outer realms . . . Only here can you get the full meaning of horror and nameless things out of cosmic depths and of time's abyss. Here in this volume all the splendours and marvels of far-flung galaxies are laid before your eyes in an unending pageantry of weirdness . . . in this reviewer's opinion and that of many fans, Lovecraft excels Poe himself.

Printed separately by lithography and bound in *The Alchemist* 1, No. 4 (December 1940), Hunt's "Star Spawn" was a further—this time visual—tribute to *The Outsider,* in particular Virgil Finlay's beautiful dust wrapper. Finlay's seminal piece was made up of collaged bits of work done previously by him for *Weird Tales,* the *American Weekly,* and other publications. Roy's is a complete original illustration delineating that "unending pageantry of weirdness." The art ended up in the collection of one Forrest J Ackerman, who knew a good thing when he saw it.

Hunt's first professional work was an illustration for Robert W. Lowndes's Mythos tale "The Abyss" (*Stirring Science Stories,* February 1941). A non-traditional drawing of Cthulhu followed in the fanzine *Starlight* No. 1 (Spring 1941), bearing more than a passing ancestral resemblance to Ray Harryhausen's Kraken surfacing much later in *Clash of The Titans* (1981). Could Harryhausen, a confederate of early fans Ackerman and Ray Bradbury, have had access to this publication?

Roy designed a superb cover for the *Third World Science Fiction Convention* (The "Denvention") in July 1941 as well as the cover and membership cards for the Fourth ("Pacificon") held in Los Angeles (1946). Another non-traditional take on Cthulhu was done for the cover of *Fanfare* 2, No. 2 (February 1942). This was the first art by Hunt that this writer ever saw, and it is one of his most reproduced works. Printed in an ichoric emerald ink, a "vague suggestion of a Cyclopean archi-tectural" backdrop has Cthulhu in the foreground, ITS general outline less anthropomorphic than usually depicted, pos-sessing the crouching form of "a dragon . . . [with] a pulpy tentacled head" surmounting that. This version shows up again as a "bas relief" in Hunt's illustration for Lin Carter's "H. P. Lovecraft: The Books" (*Inside* No. 16, September 1956).

Hunt's two very different versions of the R'lyehian are fur-ther argument that there can, if not should, be a multitude of visions of "forms of which poetry and legend alone have caught."

3.

While working as a curator and artist at the Colorado State Historical Museum in Denver, Roy produced a series of woodcut prints on commission for the WPA (Works Progress Administration). He would use this medium in fanac going forward. The highpoint of his woodblock art had to be the cover of the first issue of the *Alchemist* published after World War II (2, No. 1) in August 1946.

A photo of Hunt published in Stanley Mullen's fanzine, the *Goryon* 2, No. 1 (August 1948), shows him in front of his bookcase. You can make out the spine of John Coleman Bur-roughs's dustjacket for his Dad's *Synthetic Men of Mars* (1940—enthusiastically reviewed by RVH in the *Alchemist* 1, No. 2, March 1940). Also on Roy's desk is a studio portrait photo of the writer A(braham) Merritt, who was an extensive correspondent with the budding artist ("There's nobody I'd rather have want my photo more than you."—Merritt to Hunt, 20 August 1941). Merritt's side of the conversation is published in Sam Moskowitz's *A. Merritt: Reflections in the Moon Pool* (Oswald Train, 1985). It is hoped that someone (FFE perhaps?) could find and reprint Hunt's letters in this dialogue. Roy apparently lobbied for Hannes Bok, acting as an intermediary, for the job of illustrating Merritt's *The Metal Monster* (1920), perhaps in a definitive edition: "Thanks for the offer on Metal Monster and full edition . . . I like the black and gold idea" (Merritt to Hunt, 11 May 1941).

We need to "hear" Roy's letters!

Like Bok, a fair amount of Hunt's art for fanzines has an Art Deco style prevalent at that time. Roy did contribute a bibliography of Merritt's work to the premiere issue of the *Gorgon* in March 1947. Covers for another fanzine of the 1940s *Le Zombie* not only show what appears to be the use of a litho crayon for additional shading, but the influence of Alexander King's voudon tableaux in William Seabrook's *Magic Island* (1929).

4.

Roy seemed foremost to be a fan of Edgar Rice Burroughs, beginning with his enjoyment of Hal Foster's adaptation of *Tarzan of the Apes* in the Sunday newspapers. Hunt aspired to "study under J. Allen St. John [ERB's main illustrator] . . . I would set about copying [pictures and colored jackets] diligently." This is especially evident in Hunt's own cover design and typography. After high school, he had worked creating handcrafted marquees for theaters. His lettering shows the clear influence of St. John's titles for Burroughs's dustjackets (Capital T's especially looking "sword-like," not to mention St. John's iconic redesigned logo for *Weird Tales*)—a bespoke hand drawn jacket for John Taine's novel *The Gold Tooth* being the best example (and superior to the actual printed edition's design from 1927). While doing his wartime service with the US Navy, Roy actually ran into his idol ERB who was then serving as a war correspondent.

Hunt also recounted meeting the screen's first sound Tarzan, Frank Merrill, in *ERB-dom* No. 21 (July 1967). His cover for the eightieth number of that same publication is one of this writer's new favorites: a profile of *The War Chief,* Shoz Dijiji, rendered in concentric hues of a Colorado sunset. It transcends the influences of other artists, being a definitive illustration for a Burroughs work (1927) that is purely *Huntian*. I remember when this fanzine came out in 1975, I was less receptive to its cover's style, preferring something more . . . Frazetta-like? With age comes wisdom. The art of Roy V. Hunt became then more than just the sum of his influences—Lovecraft, Merritt, Burroughs, Finlay, St. John, etc.—

achieving that rare alchemy of being an inspiration to those of us who come after him.

All those book illustrations for Mullen's *Moonfoam and Sorceries* which started this appreciation are reproduced fully herein, yet one now *needs* the totality of the actual published tome in its dark blue inked silver wraps. As anyone interested in great Old School fantasy illustration also needs *Roy V. Hunt: A Retrospective*.

Spectral Voices

Leigh Blackmore

ELINOR MORDAUNT. *The Villa and the Vortex: Supernatural Stories, 1916–1924.* Edited by Melissa Edmundson. Bath, UK: Handheld Press, 2021. $17.99 tpb. ISBN 9781912766420.

Elinor Mordaunt was the legally changed pen name of the woman born Evelyn May Clowes (1872–1942). She was a prolific and popular novelist and traveler born in Nottinghamshire, England, who worked in Australia and Britain in the first thirty-five years of the twentieth century. Clowes's first book, *The Garden of Contentment,* was published in England in 1902 as by "Elinor Mordaunt." At Melbourne she published a volume of sketches, *Rosemary, That's for Remembrance* (1909), and in 1911 appeared *On the Wallaby through Victoria,* by E. M. Clowes, an interesting account of conditions in that state at that period. Her autobiography, *Sinabada,* which recounts many of her fascinating travels through a wide variety of countries including the tropics, was published in 1938.

Dr. Edmundson, the editor of this collection, has also compiled the excellent anthologies *Women's Weird: Strange Stories by Women, 1890–1940* (Handheld Press 2019) and *Women's Weird 2: More Strange Stories by Women, 1891–1937* (2020). The tales in this collection of Mordaunt's work are individually annotated by Kate Macdonald, who elucidates some contemporary slang and cant terms, place-names, and other references. Edmundson provides a thorough introduction sketching out the writer's life and work.

Mordaunt is a neglected supernatural writer. I confess my almost total unfamiliarity with her, though on looking her up in Mike Ashley and William G. Contento's superb *The Supernatural Index,* I see that a few of her stories appeared in *Hutchinson's Magazine* between 1921 and 1923, and in such anthologies as Bohun Lynch's *A Muster of Ghosts* (US edition as *Best Ghost Stories*) and C. A Dawson Scott's *Twenty and*

Three Stories (both 1924). ("Hodge" from the Scott anthology is reprinted in Edmundson's earlier *Women's Weird* volume.)

After a lapse of fifty or so years, in more modern times, a few editors of the 1970s and 1980s reprinted tales by her: Claire Necker chose her tale "The Yellow Cat" for reprint in *Supernatural Cats* (1972); J. J. Strating reprinted her "The Recall" in *Sea Tales of Terror* (1974; it was also reprinted in Rick Ferreira's 1978 anthology *A Chill to the Sunlight*); Peter Smith reprinted her "Mrs Scarr" in *The Haunted Sea* (1975); Bill Wannan reprinted her early tale "The Skipper's Yarn" in his *Australian Horror Stories* (1983); and Richard Dalby reprinted "The Landlady" in his *Virago Book of Ghost Stories: The Twentieth Century: Volume Two* (1991), a.k.a. *Modern Ghost Stories by Eminent Women Writers* (1992–96). Her tale "The High Seas" appears in Mike Ashley's recent *From the Depths and Other Strange Tales of the Sea* (British Library, 2018).

Tales of Elinor Mordaunt (Martin Secker, 1934) is an omnibus of tales drawn from her previous short story collections and is now rare. Most of the stories in the present collection are taken from *Tales. The Villa and the Vortex* provides a welcome reintroduction of a body of this writer's work in the supernatural and fantastic. What we have in the volume under consideration is a solid collection of nine fantastic tales from Mordaunt's pen, a number of them unavailable for many years: "The Weakening Point," "The Country-side," "The Vortex," "Hodge," "The Fountain," "Luz," "The Landlady," "Four Wallpapers" and "The Villa."

More than one contemporary reviewer compared the strength of Mordaunt's bleak and hard-edged writing, which nevertheless focusses on questions of personal evil and supernatural forces at play in the world, to the writings of Algernon Blackwood.

Loneliness, pagan sacrifice, the consequences of fear and obsession (as in "The Vortex" with its playwright who must achieve success no matter what the price), are all featured in Mordaunt's work as origins or causes of haunting. The liminal nature of certain forces is well articulated in "Hodge," with its being or spirit who is never quite able to incarnate or fully emerge into the world of those who "discover" him.

Yet sometimes Mordaunt's tales verge on the scientific realms of an H. G. Wells, as in the crazed scientist motif in "Luz," where fear once again plays an integral role, but the central character suffers from a hubris that often overtakes those who dare trifle with the very stuff of life and death itself. In "The Landlady," notions of "ghost" are complicated by the quotidian into being interpretable as aspects of what lies all around us on a daily basis—another parallel with the mysticism of a Blackwood.

"The Countryside" is perhaps Mordaunt's most potent tale in the volume—a story of folk magic and witchcraft let loose upon the realm of parochial religion with all its usual hallmarks of repression. Witchcraft here marks out the freedom of women's ways and rebellion against the theological forces that would seek to constrain them within a straitjacket of conventional morality. In "The Fountain," Welsh legendry, mermaids, and the heritage of ancient Druidry come into play in a whirlwind of fate which catches up its characters in a net of seemingly inescapable magic. Mordaunt also excels in a story of prophetic dreams such as "The Weakening Point."

The editor concludes her well-researched biographical and critical introduction with the "sincere hope that this present volume of Elinor Mordaunt's supernatural fiction will allow her work to take its place within women's literary history and within the tradition of supernatural fiction." We concur with this hope, and look forward to more of Elinor Mordaunt's accomplished supernatural fiction being collected from the short story collections where it lies unjustly forgotten.

Meanwhile, you will not regret obtaining *Villa and Vortex* if you are a devotee of the ghostly and spectral.

Who Is Anybody?

Géza A. G. Reilly

RAMSEY CAMPBELL. *Somebody's Voice*. London & New York: Flame Tree Press, 2021. 343 pp. $14.95 tpb. ISBN: 9781787586062.

I quailed a little bit when I started reading Ramsey Campbell's new novel, *Somebody's Voice*. The book came out shortly after the height of the imbroglio between the trans community and certain renowned English writers, and I was legitimately concerned that Campbell's newest venture would be diving into that particular political morass. Since I have a deep respect and admiration for his writing, that wasn't a road I wanted to see him walk down. Campbell is no stranger to uncomfortable ideas in his fiction that correspond to real-world issues, and he inevitably handles them with deftness and care. In this instance, however, I was concerned that he would end up as one more name on the cancelling pile. Thankfully, though there are political elements in *Somebody's Voice,* the novel is less invested in politics than it is in matters of identity and communication.

Somebody's Voice is the story of successful true-crime writer Alex Grand. Alex has fallen on some hard times because his most recent book deals with issues of child abuse and matters relevant to the trans community. Put simply, he is being taken to task for writing of experiences that he has never had himself. At the proverbial cusp of failure, Alex is thrown a lifeline: he is given the chance to ghostwrite the story of Carl Batchelor, a trans man who presents a compelling narrative about surviving childhood sexual abuse and growing into a realization of gender identity. Although this goes well for them both at first, the path to success becomes twisted over time, throwing Alex into a maelstrom of confusion, lies, and torturous concepts of truth and falsity.

In this novel, Campbell is at the height of his powers when

it comes to crafting dialogue. There has been a sense in Campbell's novels over the past decade or two that he has a primary interest in the impossibility of communication. Very few expressions between persons are comprehended and accepted at face value, and true understanding in conversation seems to be an ever-retreating ideal. Dialogue is less of an exchange of information between individuals and more a minefield filled with shadows and fog. In Campbell's fiction, honest communication seems to fail in the face of cruel assumptions, and if there is the chance of a catastrophic *mis*communication, that chance will become a certainty.

This sense of the impossibility of communication runs throughout *Somebody's Voice,* and it infects the very idea of writing as a means of expression. After all, Alex has no firsthand knowledge of what he writes about—perhaps—but does that make his books any less meaningful or honest? If he does have some experience of his subject matter, does that lend his work a legitimacy it would otherwise be bereft of? What of Carl, Alex's ghostwriting subject? Carl's story is contested at several points in the novel—does its truth or falsity make a difference to its significance? *Somebody's Voice* plays with these questions but fittingly never truly answers them. Looking for a bedrock of truth, an anchor point upon which we can securely rest our trust, is a futile quest in a recent Campbell novel. There is in his worlds only chaos pretending to be civilized, and underneath it all is a dominion of doubt, misunderstanding, and distrust.

I was reminded of some of Umberto Eco's fiction by *Somebody's Voice*. Eco wrote fairly consistently of the truth-in-falsity and the falsity-in-truth. It permeated his novels and was, for me, a highpoint of his narrative style. Campbell takes a similar approach, only his concern is interpersonal rather than ontological. Nobody really *is* anybody in this novel; identities are temporarily fixed more by stubborn habit than they are by any inherent sense of social or even personal truth. This is, naturally, exemplified in Alex, who as a writer is used to the internal adoption of a multitude of equally valid—and often conflicting—identities. But it is present in every character to one degree or another, whether it entails a simple and minor change in a name or a drastic overhaul of the memories one has of another. Flux, rather than fixity, rules the internal and external lives of these characters to no small amount of horror.

Of course, *Somebody's Voice* is more of a thriller than a horror novel, or at least it would have to be pigeonholed as non-supernatural horror if one were pressed on the matter. I've never cared as much for Campbell's non-supernatural work as I have his outright supernatural novels and stories (though it must be said that *The Face that Must Die,* an early thriller, is a masterpiece of the genre). *Somebody's Voice* grabbed me almost instantly, however. I quite enjoy—and am terrified by—the direction Campbell has taken with his interest in the breakdown of communication and the impossibility of truth in interpersonal relationships. *Somebody's Voice* feels like the culmination of more than a few intellectual and emotional ideas that he has been toying with over the past few years, and expressing those ideas in a non-supernatural mien seems to give them even greater weight than they would have otherwise possessed.

This is not to say that Campbell's new novel is flawless, however, and I must admit that I'm left wondering about his representation of trans persons and trans lives. Yes, this is horribly ironic, because I'm proverbially wringing my hands over the very issue that is the inciting incident of—and an ongoing incident throughout—*Somebody's Voice*. It certainly *seems* as if Campbell handles his subjects with kindness and authenticity, and I want to be clear that I do not personally see anything of concern in how he has written the world of this novel or presented his characters. Nevertheless, I have seen others murmur about these issues in a vague manner, and thus I have to admit that people more invested in issues of gender identity and expression than my not-invested-at-all position may encounter things within *Somebody's Voice* that disturb them for all the wrong reasons. With luck, Campbell won't end up on the roster of the cancelled, and I don't think he will, but it must be said that some might find things in this novel that would simply be invisible to me.

And, thus, the impossibility of communication comes round again. Should Campbell be taken to task in the manner that his protagonist is? I certainly don't think so, but then, I'd rather not live in the nightmare realm where no one can effectively say anything of substance to another and be reliably heard. That, I think, is the point of *Somebody's Voice,* and it is felt with awesome, gripping power by the time of its rather poignant conclusion. We in life want to know ourselves, but more so, we want *other people* to know and understand us. If that simple, human yearning cannot be attained, then how can there be any reality to our own understanding of ourselves? It's quite possible that a fact that cannot be communicated is not a fact at all. And if we cannot say who *we* are with any certainty, then how can we ever presume to know others? Nothing but vague territories lay at the feet of Campbell's characters, and the depth of those territories invites paralysis far more than exploration. Would that we never have to step within the engaging, horrific morass of identity represented in *Somebody's Voice*.

Green Hell

Michael D. Miller

The Green Knight. David Lowry, dir. 2021. A24.

I am not sure if the anonymous poet of *Sir Gawain and the Green Knight* ever imagined the epic as a tale of horror, but this cinematic retelling by writer/director David Lowry is rife with philosophical, religious, and folk horror consciousness for the medieval and modern mind. On the same note, I am not sure if Lowry thinks that way about the film either, considering his past credits, *Empire Builder* (2014), *Pete's Dragon* (2016), and *The Old Man and the Gun* (2018). Given that this film is an adaptation of a medieval poem, looking into the theories behind the form may shed some light on these uncertainties. (Note: please be aware, this review contains spoilers!)

The agency of film adaptation is best understood through analyzing the artist's and critic's approach as best described in Karen Kline's idea of "Four Critical Paradigms of Film Adaptation."[1] In brief, those four paradigms are: Paradigm 1: "Translation: The novel is the privileged artistic work, while the film exists to 'serve' its literary precursor." Thus, the "translation paradigm" also privileges "traditionally literary elements while minimizing specifically cinematic elements, and . . . value[s] similarities rather than differences between the written and cinematic texts." Paradigm 2: "Pluralist: A successful film adaptation presents 'analogies' between the novel and the film . . . Differences between film and literature are 'acceptable,' but 'similarities are expected as well'—thus, a 'successful' film adaptation must 'find a 'balance' between these two opposing tendencies." Paradigm 3: "Transformation: First, scholars adopting this approach consider the novel and the film to be

---

1. K. Kline, "The Accidental Tourist on Page and on Screen: Interrogating Normative Theories about Film Adaptation," *Literature Film Quarterly* 24, No. 1 (1996): 70–83.

separate, autonomous arts, constituted by different sign systems. Finding equivalencies between the two systems is not a priority, and, indeed, may not be possible according to this paradigm. Second, critics adopting this paradigm often end up privileging the cinematic text over its literary source in their commentary." Paradigm 4: "Materialist: Critics adopting this approach examine the film as the product of cultural-historical processes. Materialist critics [and filmmakers] may consider give much less weight to whether or not the film adaptation is comparable to the original literary work." Let's see where this takes us with *The Green Knight*.

The original Middle-English epic poem is considered to be an attempt to go to back to the alliterative style of the early Old English poems (like *Beowulf*) and invigorate the "Arthurian Romance" tradition that, by the time this poem was written, was already seen as the stale product of a disappearing past. The poet then was taking an old genre and revising it with a look to the future. The particular Arthurian tale of Sir Gawain and his challenge to the Green Knight also includes brushes with the supernatural and pagan past, more characteristic of the early Old English poems and far away from the fourteenth century, when the poem was composed. In this sense the poem is bringing back the tropes of magic, monsters, horror, the weird, and more, from the beginning of the Middle Ages to their very end. Thematically, the poem is clear as a Christian morality tale, focusing on chastity, humility, and pride. Over time, modern fascination has been on the beheading game (a standard trope in Arthurian romances), and the conflict between Sir Gawain and his immortal nemesis the Green Knight, rather than the philosophical dimensions of the poem. Previous film adaptations such as *Sword of the Valiant* (1984) exemplify this, while *The Green Knight* (2021) subverts such conventions. The game itself is simple. The Green Knight enters Arthur's court, challenges a knight to slice off his head and, if he lives, he is allowed a retributive slice of the head of the challenger. Gawain accepts the challenge and slices off the Green Knight's head, only to see the body pick up the severed head, mount his horse, laugh, and promise to return in a year's time. Gawain knows he is doomed, but must honor his knightly promise.

So is the film a "translation"? In the original poem, the plot is broken down into three beats, the Green Knight's arrival at the court and challenge to Sir Gawain on Christmas Eve, then, a year later, a night spent in Sir Bertilak's Castle and finally, the confrontation in the Green Chapel. Our major characters are Gawain (Dev Patel), the Green Knight (Ralph Ineson), the Lord (Joel Edgerton), his Lady (Alicia Vikander), King Arthur (Sean Harris), and Morgan le Fay (Sarita Choudhury). While the film has these elements, it has little else. The journey to the Green Chapel is significantly expanded with encounters not in the poem, and these are what moves the story in a more horrific, supernatural, and weird atmosphere. Looking at these elements certainly sets up a pluralist consideration of the film's intent.

Sir Gawain and the Green Knight, the poem, reads well on paper and is filled with verbose description and strange magical practices and customs. For example, Gawain's shield is outfitted with a pentacle, which in the poem is not a mystical symbol in its own right but represents "the eternal knot," a symbol of perfection, befitting Gawain's status as the best knight of the round table. Yet the poem lacks the action that a modern audience would demand. Lowry gives us three key "action" scenes on Gawain's journey. Early on his lonely journey on horseback Gawain is accosted by three bandits who promptly relieve him of armor, sword, shield, and horse. Never occurring in the poem, this incident immerses the audience into the world. Gawain is mortal, in peril, and unlikely to make his meeting with the Green Knight. Next, Gawain finds a remote house haunted by the spirit of a decapitated woman, whose head rests in the bottom of the lake. Taking a more horrific turn with this interlude, Gawain is able to unite the head and body, ending the curse. Lastly, Gawain is joined by a talking fox (Patrick Duffy), the weirdest of the interludes, and while encamped on a mountain cliff he watches in awe and terror as a parade of giants walk through an adjacent valley. These elements, however, hardly serve to make the film any more entertaining, but instead get us deeper into Gawain's character, slowly revealing how much of a "true" knight he may be.

At this point it is clear that Lowry's vision is more about transformation. The film certainly is the focus, not so much the poem. The cinematography is stunning, contrasting a desolate and enchanted countryside against gray and dimly lit castles. This film is much more about the experience of imagery and implication, than clear storytelling. It is also evident that Lowry is subverting much of the literary mode and theme of the poem's character. The opening image presents Gawain as king, his crown looking more like a medieval torture device, followed by a pagan chant against his "chastity"; the image then burns, making Gawain seem a sacrificial wicker man. The chanting voice is Morgan le Fay, whose role in Arthurian romance is to destroy Arthur's knight's chastity. In the poem, Morgan is Gawain's aunt; in the film, his mother. In the poem, Gawain never doubts himself until the end; in the film Gawain is always questioning and uncertain. It is a "human" Gawain, not an idealized hero. In the castle of Sir Bertilak, where his lady tests Gawain's chastity and humility three times, Gawain fails, and knows it. In the poem, Gawain holds true. Magic enters the film via a green girdle. In the poem, Bertilak's lady gives this to Gawain; in the film, it is Gawain's mother who gives the girdle. The significance is that the girdle will protect Gawain from the Green Knight's axe. The theme is: does one cheat death and use the girdle, or be true and take the blow of the axe without magical aid? Here both Gawains are the same: they love, and want to live, to the point of cheating. Where the film disappoints is the Green Knight's composure. Although clearly representing nature and testing the virtue of knighthood, this villain comes off looking more like an Ent from Peter Jackson's *Lord of the Rings* in armor. Also lost are the subtle hints: Bertilak is the Green Knight (nature) and the Lady is Morgan (paganism) testing Gawain his entire stay.

While it seems clear Lowry is creating a separate experience from the poem, there may be some materialist impressions in the journey. What would they be, though? What cultural critique might be served by this atmospheric medieval tale? Looking at the beginning and ending may point that out. The film opens with Gawain in a brothel on Christmas Eve; he claims to love the harlot he is with. Already we have an unchaste knight, completely upending a traditional portrayal of Gawain. And the end, the climatic beheading in the Green Chapel? In the poem, Gawain cheats, uses the green girdle, and survives with just a nick. He returns and confesses to his fellow knights and remits himself from the order. But they embrace him, confessing they would have done the same, wearing green girdles from that day on in Gawain's honor. In the film, as the axe blade lowers, we go into a sweeping vision of Gawain's future, all the pain, misery, wars, famine, and plague his future will comprise. A life of suffering and loss. Gawain removes the girdle. If this is not a cultural material critique, what is it? Are we a less Christian people? More willing to learn that death is better than life? That we can't live up to it? A Ligottian hell, where the logical fallacy of life itself is subverted by Gawain's embrace of death?

The Green Knight casts an ominous spell with folk horror elements in the formula. Brothels, sex as a rite, mysterious other faiths, even King Arthur's costume and crown design: there is a constant reminder of a crown of thorns (one perhaps we all wear) and removing the glamor of "shining armor" and Camelot pageantry to its simple roots, a king in a hall, surrounded by a band of men. The round table in this hall is an incomplete circle, leaving an opening for those wishing to address the king to advance to the center. The film keeps the spirit of the Middle Ages, yet changes the theme and character of the poem. The Gawain poet was a revisionist wanting to go back to the past to see the present differently. Lowry follows the same intent with his film. Like Robert Eggers's *The Lighthouse* (2019), *The Green Knight* is ultimately a weird revisionist work that is folk tradition versus religion (modern), pagan versus Christian (medieval), with philosophical (cosmic) implications of meaninglessness. The film, like the poem, remains a morality tale, once an epic romance, now weird and horrific!

Treats and Tricks

Tony Fonseca

ELLEN DATLOW, ed. *The Best Horror of the Year, Volume 13*. New York: Night Shade Books. 2021. 384 pp. $15.99 tpb. ISBN 9781949102604.

Hugo-winning editor Ellen Datlow has been called "the venerable queen of horror anthologies" by the *New York Times*. Albeit a bit hyperbolic, this is well-deserved praise, since Datlow has been one of the movers and shakers of horror literature for more than three decades. And just in time for Halloween, she has edited the thirteenth volume of *The Best Horror oy the Year*, which includes one poem and twenty-four stories that range in length from 3100 to 12,000 words. She notes in her preface that among other concerns, she strove for diversity: fourteen of the stories are by men, while nine are by women, with contributors are from U.S., U.K., Thailand, Italy, and Canada. The volume's prefatory material also includes a summary of awards for the year (e.g., the Horror Writers Association Bram Stoker Awards, the Shirley Jackson Awards, and the World Fantasy Awards). Datlow also includes a helpful list of notable 2020 novels, chapbooks and novellas, anthologies, mixed-genre anthologies, collections, and mixed-genre collections, as well as magazines, journals, and webzines, mixed-genre magazines. Her list also includes artists and nonfiction.

As far as the short stories in the volume are concerned, let's just say they are somewhat of a mixed bag, with some absolute treats (including my new favorite horror short story), some could-have-been great stories if only . . . , some tales that missed the mark, and some downright tricks—stories by authors who use a horror trope but would also have to use pretzel logic to call the work horror.

I'll begin with two of the best works in the volume, Alessandro Manzetti's "Bloody Rhapsody" and Sarah Pinsker's

"Two Truths and a Lie." Manzetti's brief poem about Jack the Ripper is one of the best horror-themed poems I have read (to be honest, it's a subgenre that I am not that fond of, so finding a masterful horror poem is a treat). Manzetti employs unforgettable imagery, creates a wonderful eerie atmosphere, and is a thoughtful and thought-provoking treatment of the topic. Pinsker's story is also masterful and now ranks as my all-time favorite horror tale. It's a truly disquieting, wickedly eerie, well-paced, meticulously constructed, and unpredictable text that pulls no punches and, more importantly, ends exactly the way it should. It even contains a false protagonist, which is a nice touch and something writers don't do often enough. The basic premise of the story is that hoarder and recluse Denny, the older brother of our false protagonist Marco, has died, and it falls upon Marco to clean out his house, which is no mean feat. At the poorly attended funeral, Marco's estranged high school friend Stella offers (out of a sense of obligation and guilt, or so it seems, as the story is a good bit about fate) to help. The story's actual protagonist, Stella, is a pathological liar who began the practice in college in order to reinvent herself. While cleaning, she finds an old television, which causes her to make a remark about an open access show from their shared childhood, *The Uncle Bob Show* (at first she believes she's making the show up, another lie, but when Marco remembers the show, she realizes something is amiss). Marco then finds an old VHS tape of the show, a weird program where children run into an entirely black room and find bright toys in secret compartments, and as they play, Uncle Bob comes out, always staring directly into the camera, and proceeds to tell dark and disturbing fairy tales starring various children. It turns out the stories predict what happens to each of the children on the set, and Stella has repressed the fact that she was one of those children (Marco escaped the fate because he was too young). Now obsessed with this new reality, Stella investigates and discovers that Denny spent his entire life trying to find a way to escape his fate, which resulted in his hoarding; Stella's fate, however, seems locked in, as her story was about a girl who lied so much she forgot what was true, ultimately losing herself as she takes parts and memories of other people to reconstruct herself. She sets out to find Uncle Bob to avoid her fate, only to end up more lost.

Other masterful stories in the volume include A. C. Wise's "Exhalation #10," Jason Sanford's "The Eight-Thousanders," Nathan Ballingrud's "Scream Queen," and J. A. W. McCarthy's "Contrition (1998)." Wise's story is about two male college friends. One (Paul) is a homicide detective and the other (Henry) is a would-be director and ex-sound editor known for his unnatural hearing ability. The story is about Henry's being openly in love with the heterosexual and married Paul, as well as the investigation of a serial killer who tapes his victims' last breaths. Paul enlists Henry to watch a tape of a female murder victim, and Henry's hearing allows the two to find another tape of a second victim. Ultimately, his hearing allows them to find the murderer, as well as other tapes and buried bodies. The emphasis is not as much on the hunt as it is on the psychological effect the murders and tapes have on Henry and Paul, as sharing something so sorrowful causes them to grow apart. While the ending is a bit much, as Henry becomes a filmmaker and wins an Oscar, this it doesn't detract too much from the brilliance of the story or its beautifully written prose.

Sanford's "The Eight-Thousanders," my second favorite in the volume, tells the tale of two men, Keller and Ronnie, the latter being the former's jet-setter tech boss who has a taste for danger. The two are climbing Mount Everest as part of a crew, Ronnie for the first time without supplemental oxygen. When they stumble on a dying climber, they meet Ferri, a centuries-old vampire who hates killing, so feeds off the dying climbers once there is no chance that they will survive. The two make it to the top, but on the descent they find themselves in danger as a storm is approaching. Even though she knows they are likely to die, Ferri helps them find camp, but the storm lasts into a second day (it turns out that Ronnie knew the weather would be dangerous but put his crew at risk anyway). Ultimately, Keller has to leave Ronnie (who had tried to kill him earlier) behind, as he cannot continue to support him and live himself; he leaves his boss with Ferri. The story's emphasis is on Keller's friendship with the vampire, who helps him to realize his repressed motivations. It is a master class in storytelling, with a bittersweet, perfect ending, with no pulled punches, as Keller realizes that his fate is to one day die on Everest in Ferri's arms.

Ballingrud's "Scream Queen," despite a somewhat confusing open ending, is well written. One of the most horrifying in the volume, it tells the story of an aging would-be documentary producer and director (Alan) and a young hotshot camera man (Mark) as they interview elderly actress Jennifer Drummond, known for her one performance in a 1970s cult film, in which she played a possessed girl. Like so many young males who watched the film, they fell in love with her because of a nude scene. The two find out too late that she was actually possessed and has been fighting a demon for decades, having starved it; it has rotted inside her but has changed her into a demon herself, one they are fated to end up worshipping the rest of their days.

McCarthy's "Contrition (1998)" is about a cursed film that causes people to relive moments when they've hurt others, causing extreme guilt, and making some people sick, crazed, or even suicidal. The narrator (a woman named Alex) works at a movie theater that is showing the film, which draws only small crowds, but the theater owner plays it because the distributor pays him to do so (a possible foreshadowing of the story's end, which I will not give away). Eventually, Alex's coworkers, even if they get only a passing glimpse of the film, are affected: one mutilates herself out of guilt for her absence from her dead brother's life, while another, a normally sheepish young male usher, murders an abusive frat boy who constantly teases the female staff. Alex is similarly affected, causing her to see things that remind her of her most selfish and worst moments. Finally, she teams with the theater's manager to watch the entire movie. How the two decide to handle the film is a brilliant piece of writing.

Though they don't quite measure up to the complete mastery of the aforementioned stories, the volume includes many other wonderful pieces, namely Catriona Ward's "A Hotel in Germany," Maria Haskins's "Cleaver, Meat, and Block," Simon Bestwick's "A Treat for Your Last Day," and Thana Niveau's "The Whisper of Stars." The best of these, Haskins's

"Cleaver, Meat, and Block," is perhaps the most topical story in the volume, as it relates the tale of an epidemic that causes some humans to become "raveners," humanoid creatures who feast on live flesh. The action is set post-epidemic, once a vaccine has eliminated the disease and made them human again. The main character, Hannah, is a young girl whose entire family (including her dog) was eaten by one of her schoolmates' family members. She now lives with her grandparents, butchers who give her a cleaver as a gift. She has become mistrustful and reclusive, watching as ex-raveners become bullies. It is then that she begins to suspect they remember what they did, and enjoyed it, a suspicion that is secretly shared by her grandmother and later verified by her ex-schoolmate. What Hannah and her grandmother do will have readers cheering.

Catriona Ward's "A Hotel in Germany," showcases her talents as a wordsmith. In many ways, it is the most beautifully written of the tales, containing lines (about an elderly movie star) such as "These mercurial shifts of feeling make her mesmerizing on the screen. She is a clear pool in which dark fish swim." The tale is about the relationship between the two main characters, Cara and the movie star. Cara, once a vampire, has watched her kind be murdered off—unless they agree to drugs that change them, constant surveillance, and a life of being owned like a pet. She has been owned by the movie star's family for more than a century; in fact, infusions from her keep the movie star alive. The focus of the story is Cara's thoughts on freedom, family, loss, and love. The ending is perfect, a quiet, uncontrived denouement, full of both despair and hope.

Bestwick's "A Treat for Your Last Day" and Niveau's "The Whisper of Stars" both have a lot of promise, but both fail on some level to live up to it. Bestwick's narrator, a teen boy, is taken along for a family vacation to seaside towns during a week of torrential rainfall. Without warning (and proper build-up), the father, a failure at work and in life, murders the mother while the boy has run ahead to climb a summit. The father calls him back and sends him to find his mother's body in a cave. The rest of the story involves a chase and attempted murder. The story is told as a recollection and an attempt to find meaning in the event; however, it does not. Here, the engaging chase scene is just not enough to offset the lack of pacing and characterization.

Niveau's artic horror tale (five people trekking through Siberia at the end of winter, looking for valuable artifacts) suffers from a similar problem. There just isn't enough information given about the main character (Alison), her brother Sean, his partner Jeff, or the enigmatic guide Eric. Dogsled guru Olga is as flat a character as one can imagine. All we know is that Alison is awkward and socially inept, Sean is selfish and snarky, and Jeff seems like a nice guy. When the creatures finally attack, it's done off-screen. In fact, the creatures remain so nebulous that no reader is going to have the slightest idea what they are, where they come from, or why they allow one person to live, having apparently (again, the writing does not make this clear) possessed that person. I wasn't even sure if the creatures had done something similar to Eric before the action of the story. It's kind of, sort of hinted at, but that's it.

The stories that I found most disappointing are Jack Lothian's "A Deed without a Name," Stephen Graham Jones's "Lords of the Matinee," Richard Gavin's "Scolo's Bridle: A Cruelty," Gemma Files's "Come Closer," Elana Gomel's "Mine Seven," Christopher Harman's "Mouselode Maze," David Surface's "The Devil Will Be at the Door," Andrew Humphrey's "Trick of the Light," Steve Duffy's "In the English Rain," and Gary McMahon's "Tethered Dogs." The best of these are by Files, Gomel, and Harman, but each misses the mark slightly. "Come Closer" and "Mine Seven" seem rushed, with enigmatic endings that left me puzzled. Both have something going for them (Files's eerie vampire house that creeps through a neighborhood is a unique creation, and Gomel's creature that seems to be made of miners who have died in accidents is a wonderful political statement), which perhaps makes the disappointment more pronounced. Harman's story about two landscapers who find themselves working inside a haunted maze suffers from the same problem as Niveau's "The Whisper of Stars" in that it leaves too much unsaid, particularly when it comes to which characters are killed and which are spared.

On the other hand, I found very little I cared for in Jack Lothian's "A Deed without a Name," which was more *Game of Thrones* than horror, a story where it is impossible to feel anything for any character, as they are all cardboard cutouts. I wanted to like Jones's witty "Lords of the Matinee," about a set of magical movie theater headphones that let one person see another's memories, but in the end it is at best an unreliable (crazy) narrator story, and at worst it took too many short-cuts, with the narrator being much too quick to act on information any reasonable human would have questioned. I at first found Gavin's "Scolo's Bridle: A Cruelty," about a man's fascination with medieval torture devices and its effect on the neighbor he has built one for him engaging, but then it got predictable, and then it got gratuitous, full of shock value but little else, which is a pity because the story could have gone in so many other more powerful directions. Surface's "The Devil Will Be at the Door" grabbed me immediately with one of the best opening pages to any story to my recollection, but then it seemed rushed, just a way to get characters from point A to point B. Humphrey's "Trick of the Light," about a couple that vacations at a haunted seaside town and meets, um, well, it's never clear what they meet (or why they meet their fate), is full of vagueness that works like a pulled punch, lessening any impact. Duffy's "In the English Rain," about a haunted house John Lennon once lived in, has the same rushed feel, and ultimately it is at best an unreliable narrator story. Finally, McMahon's "Tethered Dogs" is just a wordy rumination (albeit with an excellent horror trope) on it being better not to know the circumstances of our own deaths ahead of time.

And that brings me to the tricks, those stories that were so marginally horror that if they were included in any other collection, no one would have known they were horror. Ironically, as stories in and of themselves, two of these were some of the better-written in the volume. The always clever Michael Marshall Smith has fun with readers in "It Doesn't Feel Right," a darkly comic tale that gives a slight nod to a horror trope but is really about the dubious joys of parenting. He uses a very nice tongue-in-cheek narration to paint the picture of a father who, try as he might, cannot get his son ready for school on time because the child insists on taking off his socks. Since we all know a child or ten who has done this, the story does branch out to be about not one evil pair of socks, but a pandemic of them. Stephen Volk's "Sicko" is a re-imaging of Hitchcock's *Psycho,* told from the point of view of Marian Crane. I am tempted to call it a scholarly close reading of the film, written as a short story. Here, Marian is not murdered, and the only monsters are her boss and lover; the former blackmails her into sex, and the latter attempts to get her to use her body to blackmail her boss. Marian decides to cut both out of her life, and in an interesting twist, as she drives away, she gets stopped by a female state trooper (a stop that mirrors her earlier run-in with the male trooper).

On the other hand, three of the stories were tricks on two levels—they were only marginally horror, and they were unimpressive. The best moment in Sam Hicks's "Heath Crawler" is the narrator's frantic search for his lost dog. The story's horror tropes, a mysterious old man who may or may not be turning humans into animals (vagueness rearing its ugly head again here) and an equally mysterious Eastern European woman who tries to protect the narrator, just seem to be there as part of the background. Worse yet, nothing actually happens. Tom Johnstone's "Let Your Hinged Jaw Do the Talking" uses ventriloquist dolls as a horror trope, but the only horrifying act is the narrator's burning down her father's warehouse (full of such dolls) and then letting her uncle go to prison for it. The dolls are really just a vehicle to tell the story of how a young girl comes to understand her mother better and learns to dislike her father, who she realizes is controlling. Again, what we have here is at best an unreliable narrator story. Worse yet, when all is said and done, the story is much ado about nothing. Pete W. Sutton's "We Do Like to Be Beside" is at first highly engaging and wonderfully eerie. A family goes to the beach, but their usual spot is taken by their weird neighbors (the young narrator's sister calls the mother of the weird family a witch). The narrator goes off to find a new spot, which he does, right next to the old one, but when he comes back over the dune he cannot find his father, mother, or sister, and sees only one of the neighbor children and the weird father. This goes on for a bit, and just when I was prepared for an impactful revelation, the boy finds his mother, who tells him that he never had a sister and his father had died some time before. Worse yet, she says it was all a dream.

Weak stories aside, *The Best Horror of the Year, Volume 13* is a worthwhile pursuit for any horror reader, or for that matter, any reader, considering the excellent quality of some of the stories. As I mentioned before, some of these stories are so meticulously constructed, and some of the writing so masterful, they could serve as a master class on storytelling.

About the Contributors

Michael Abolafia is a co-editor of *Dead Reckonings*.

Leigh Blackmore is the official editor of the international Sword and Sorcery and Weird Fiction Terminus amateur press association. His recent weird verse has appeared in issues of *Penumbra* and in the *Speculations III* anthology from Mind's Eye Publications. Forthcoming work includes the liner notes for a vinyl record album from Cadabra Records, and his occult thriller novel *The Eighth Trigram*. Leigh runs his own copyediting and manuscript assessment company, Proof Perfect Editorial Services, based in the Illawarra region, NSW.

Ramsey Campbell is an English horror fiction writer, editor, and critic who has been writing for well over fifty years. He is frequently cited as one of the leading writers in the field. His website is www.ramseycampbell.com.

Dave Felton is a copy editor at Cadabra Records and an illustrator of weird fiction.

Tony Fonseca is the library director at Elms College, in Chicopee, Massachusetts. He has published (under the name Anthony J. Fonseca) several books and articles on horror and dark literature, horror film, academic librarianship, musical film, and hip hop/rap music, and he co-owns the independent studio Dapper Kitty Music, which specializes in indie and meditative music.

Alex Houstoun is a co-editor of *Dead Reckonings*. He has published *Copyright Questions and the Stories of H. P. Lovecraft*, available by contacting him at deadreckoningsjournal@gmail.com.

Karen Joan Kohoutek, an independent scholar and poet, has published about weird fiction in various journals and literary websites. Recent and upcoming publications have been on subjects including the Gamera films, the Robert E. Howard/H. P. Lovecraft correspondence, folk magic in the novels of Ishmael Reed, and the proto-Gothic writer Charles Brockden Brown. She lives in Fargo, North Dakota.

Javier A. Martinez was managing editor of *Extrapolation* for fifteen years. A former department chair, college dean, and university provost, he is currently professor of English in the Department of Literatures and Cultural Studies at the University of Texas Rio Grande Valley.

Michael D. Miller is a former professor of genre studies, currently active writing reviews, articles, and poetry for the weird fiction genre with work appearing in *Dead Reckonings, Lovecraft Annual, Spectral Realms, Penumbra, Alien Buddha Press, Dumpster Fire Press,* and *Marchxness.* He is the author of the *Realms of Fantasy PRG* for Mythopoeia Games Publications.

Daniel Pietersen writes cultural criticism on all aspects of horror and Gothic, is a regular guest lecturer for the Romancing the Gothic project and is also the editor of *I Am Stone: The Gothic Weird of R. Murray Gilchrist* for the British Library's Tales of the Weird series. Dan lives in a very old house in Edinburgh with his wife and dog. He is on Twitter at @pietersender.

June Pulliam teaches courses about slasher films and zombies at Louisiana State University in Baton Rouge, where she lives in an old house with multiple cats and dogs. She is the author of several books on subjects ranging from zombies to punk rock. When she is not dodging hurricanes, she paints.

Dan Raskin lives in Minneapolis, Minnesota, where he writes weird fiction and records noise electronics. He also co-hosts *The Unseen Book Club,* a podcast about narrative texts, history, and radical politics.

Dr. Géza A. G. Reilly is a writer and critic with an interest in twentieth-century American genre literature. A Canadian expatriate, he now lives in the wilds of Florida with his wife, Andrea, and their cat, Mim.

Darrell Schweitzer is an American writer, editor (formerly of *Weird Tales*), and critic, most of whose work falls into the darker part of the fantasy spectrum. PS Publishing recently published a two-volume retrospective of his work.

Joe Shea (The joey Zone) is an artist and illustrator. Samples of his work can be found at www.joeyzoneillustration.com.

Hank Wagner is a respected critic and journalist. Among the many publications in which his work regularly appears are *Cemetery Dance* and *Mystery Scene*.

www.ingramcontent.com/pod-product-compliance
Lightning Source LLC
Chambersburg PA
CBHW061744020426
42331CB00006B/1355